DRIFTING HOME

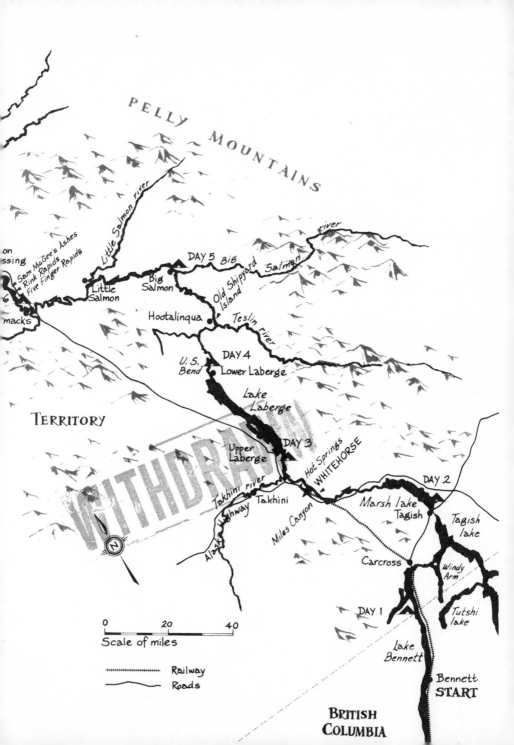

PIERRE
BERTON

DRIFTING
HOME

A FAMILY'S VOYAGE OF DISCOVERY
DOWN THE WILD YUKON RIVER

Douglas & McIntyre
VANCOUVER/TORONTO

Douglas & McIntyre
2323 Quebec Street, Suite 201
Vancouver, British Columbia V5T 4S7
www.douglas-mcintyre.com

National Library of Canada Cataloguing in Publication Data

Berton, Pierre, 1920–
Drifting home

ISBN 1-55054-951-0

1. Berton, Pierre, 1920– 2. Yukon Territory—Description and travel.
3. Yukon River (Yukon and Alaska)—Description and travel.
4. Yukon Territory—History—1895-* I. Title.

FC4017.3.B47 2002   917.19'1043   C2002-910644-3
FI091.B47 2002

Cover design by Val Speidel
Cover photo by Paul Souders/Getty Images

Printed and bound in Canada by Friesens
Printed on acid-free paper

The publisher gratefully acknowledges the financial support of the Canada Council
for the Arts, the British Columbia Ministry of Tourism, Small Business and
Culture, and the Government of Canada through the Book Publishing Industry
Development Program (BPIDP) for its publishing activities.

DAY ONE

We begin at the beginning, at Lake Bennett where the Yukon river rises and where, on a perfect June day in 1898, seven thousand hand-made boats of every conceivable structure and design set off under sail, paddle and sweep for the Klondike goldfields on an adventure which my family and I hope to recapture.

We have come up from Skagway on the Alaskan coast by narrow-gauge railway through the White Pass where the horses died by the thousands and where you can still see the authentic trail of '98, no more than the ghost of a footpath now, hammered into the clay and shale by the tramp of metal shoes and hobnailed boots seventy-four years before. Ahead of us lie six hundred miles of Yukon river system, including four lakes, a canyon, two sets of rapids, sixteen ghost settlements and, at the end of the voyage, my old home town of Dawson. I am going back to my roots; my children are going back with me.

We are standing on the Bennett station platform, looking for our baggage and peering between the coaches out at the choppy lake. I have seen the lake when the wind is asleep and the colour is a brilliant green and the surface so polished that the encircling mountains sweep down to the shoreline to join their mirror image. But now a stiff breeze has darkened the water.

The only visible reminder of the goldrush days is the little church that stands on a promontory at the head of the lake, a simple structure of unpeeled logs, with no floor and scarcely any history because the stampede rolled past it before it could be completed. This deserted log building is probably the most photographed religious structure in Canada: thousands of tourists have taken their cameras to the rocks above the church, carefully placing the spire against the backdrop of lake and mountains. Until today I thought there had never been a service held in the Bennett church. Now, however, a railway official tells my wife, Janet, that there has been a wedding just two days before—a wedding that went on all night, with two hundred guests camped out in the rain to the music of a rock group. "They had to stand up on the train all the way back to Skagway and they was pretty wet from the rain but that music never stopped playing. It was some wedding. You'll never ever see a wedding like it." The idea of the wedding charms and fascinates Janet; she would like to climb the hill and look over the church but there is no time. She must locate the boxes of provisions we shipped from the East several weeks ago.

There are several hundred people at the Bennett railway station on this August noon hour but only a few are able to see the church or the lake. The station has been cunningly situated so that the tracks lie between the scenery and the lunchroom. Two trains, one from Skagway, Alaska, and the other from Whitehorse, Yukon, effectively block the view. The tourists emerging from lunch must either walk around the trains or clamber illegally between the cars as they unbutton their camera cases and discuss the luncheon they have just finished. Was it moosemeat? they ask themselves. The waitresses have refused to confirm or deny that rumour. So it *must* have been moosemeat!

I have eaten at the Bennett lunchroom more than a dozen times over the past half-century and always there has been this rumour about moosemeat. In fact I used to tell the tourists they were eating moosemeat and half-believed it myself, even though I have eaten enough good moosemeat to know the difference between the real thing and beef cooked black and soaked in gravy. But the rumour persists and the staff encourages it. Why not? It is a harmless fancy.

Far down on the wooden platform, Janet spots a hillock of familiar cardboard boxes and sighs with relief. There are nineteen of them and they represent a triumph of logistics. That pile includes eleven boxes of food, each containing a day's rations and carefully marked from DAY ONE to DAY ELEVEN in block letters. For weeks, it seems to me, our dining room and kitchen floors were covered with these boxes and their contents as Janet and Pamela, my second daughter, pored over the daily menus and worked and reworked the lists of paraphernalia that would be needed for the trip: cooking utensils, asbestos mitts, tongs, knives, J-cloths, spices, condiments.

"I know we've left something out," Janet would say in her cheerful manner. "I just *know* it," and then she would shrug and say "Oh, well, can't be helped" and Pamela, who is so much like her, would shrug with her. "It won't be the end of the world, Mom," Pamela would say.

Now the two of them walk down the platform to survey the stack of provisions. Much of it has been bruised in three thousand miles of travel. Some of the boxes have been damaged; the string is gone; the cardboard is battered and torn. One or two have sprung open. "It could have been worse," Janet says. She counts the boxes carefully, checking them against her list. One seems to be lost but neither she nor Pamela can be sure. Did they send an extra box at the last

9

moment? Or was it *two* extra boxes? Those last days became a little hectic. "Oh, well," Janet says, shrugging once more, "if something goes missing we can always blame it on the lost box."

In addition to the provisions on the platform, a small mountain of personal luggage – twenty-two separate pieces – has to be hoisted out of the baggage car; when these are stacked next to the nineteen boxes of provisions, they make an awesome pile. How can all this gear and provender – and fourteen people – be packed into three rubber rafts?

That is Skip Burns' problem and he contemplates it with his usual good humour. Skip is the Skagway outfitter who will take us down the river. At the moment, he and his two helpers are pumping up the rafts. He is a lean and raw-boned American in his late twenties, with a Klondike mustache, a shock of red hair, a southern accent, and a brand new bride, Cheri, who works as one of the helpers.

"Congratulations, Skip. When'd you get married?"

"Just two days ago. Right up there."

"In the church? That was *you?*"

"That was us – it was some wedding. Wasn't it, Cheri?"

Cheri smiles. She is 23, with blue eyes and freckles, and she reminds me of those Yukon saplings that grow along the edges of the creeks; I met her last year when she was working as a packer for Skip on the Chilkoot Pass. While we gasped under our twenty-five pound packs she shouldered sixty and tripped over the mountains like a schoolgirl.

"Going to be a tight fit," Skip says, as we begin to load the rafts. He has not realized what big eaters we are. He ordinarily supplies the food for his regular river safaris – much of it freeze-dried, light to pack and quick to prepare. But we are a hungry lot and we want to enjoy the meals as well as the scenery, so we have contracted with Skip to supply all that is needed *except* food. Those cartons contain everything from double smoked hams to Ontario cheeses – enough to last at least fourteen people for eleven days – a total of 462 meals. No wonder Skip scratches his head as the rafts sink lower and lower into the water.

"I'm going to have to take on a freight canoe at Whitehorse – that's all there is to it," Skip tells me. "That means we're going to need an extra pilot."

The three rubber rafts – I think of them now as boats, for they have high sides and pointed prows – are riding very low. Skip turns to a buddy of his, who has come up on the train with us from Skagway. His name is Ross Miller and he is heading for Atlin where he will join his father, a noted glaciologist, doing experimental summer work on the vast Mendenhall Glacier. When Skip made his first river trip down the Yukon some years ago – a kind of dry run for his outfitting business – Ross was one of a group of Alaskan Boy Scouts he took with him.

Ross is standing off to one side, waiting for the train to move on. He is wearing tweed knickers and low Oxfords, scarcely the proper attire for a river journey. I watch as Skip walks over to him. The two talk together for a few moments, occasionally looking across at us and at the pile of provisions. Then Ross walks over to the baggage car, finds his gear and slings it into one of the boats. He has known us for a few hours only and to him we seem to be pretty much of a closed corporation. But he is an old friend of Skip and Cheri and Skip's other pilot, Scotty Jeffers, and he cannot resist another journey down the river. Now we are fifteen: four guides, two parents, five daughters, two sons, a nephew and a boyfriend. Eight of them share the same grandfather, who, three-quarters of a century ago, at the age of 27, followed this water highway for more than six hundred miles.

11

My father must have known that his chances of finding any gold were slight. But in the spring of 1898 everybody was going to the Klondike, as everybody goes off to war. Half of New Brunswick seemed to be heading northwest, taking advantage of a railway freight war to cross the continent cheaply. There were five hundred and fifty men on the train with him and most of them had never seen a mountain before. Neither had he and he was entranced. "The scenery was magnificent," he wrote to his mother in Saint John, from the Oriental Hotel in Vancouver. "Mountains rising from all sides sheer up, apparently, from the track and towering above our heads as if to fall and crush us. In one place we circled around the base of a mountain in the sharpest and longest curve (for the sharpness of it) that I ever saw. The train doubled on itself, the engine being out of sight the whole time around the base of the mountain. We actually went around three-quarters of a circle before resuming our general direction. I stayed on the platform all day scarcely taking time for my meals and nearly froze to death for it was very cold."

How like him, I thought, when I came across that letter in my mother's effects. The bitterest cold could not have deterred that infinitely curious man from examining the wonders that he always saw around him. What was commonplace to his fellows was miraculous to him. He had to know how things worked and he was forever examining objects, natural or man-made, to see what made them tick and then explaining them to others. That trip through the mountains "was well worth the money twice over," he wrote. He could not get over it and in his long letter to his mother described everything he saw in meticulous detail: the Selkirk Loop, "one of the most curious sights on the journey;" a perpendicular pinnacle of naked granite that towered above him "almost blending with the pale blue of the sky and gleaming in the sun – a spectacle of inconceivable grandeur"; the famous timber bridge over Stoney Mountain creek, then the highest on the continent. While his fellow goldseekers were inside, playing cards, he was on the platform, shivering away, carefully counting the tunnels (twenty) and the snowsheds (fifty-three) and noting everything for his mother: the miners at work along the sandbars of the Fraser; the curious pulley that took men across the river in a basket; and the uncanny effect created when the train emerged from a tunnel so that "sometimes it would look like Dante's Inferno with the smoke issuing from the mouth and hiding the exit." (He knew his Dante as he knew his Virgil and his Homer and his Shakespeare.) It was a journey he never forgot and it often came back to him. Words, he said, could not describe the beauty and magnificence of it. He had almost half a century left to live and it would be spent among mountains like these, far from the Atlantic's shore, but in all those years he would repeat that journey only twice. He believed he was going to the Yukon for a two-year stay but those two years lengthened into forty. The decision to join the stampede changed the current of his life, as it changed that of so many others.

"It's weird," Peter says. "I mean, to think that he was on this lake. I wonder if he ever figured us kids would be doing it?"

We have pushed off from the shore and are chugging into the wind, heading for a patch of bright sky in the distance between the mountains and beyond the clouds. A light rain is clouding the Prussian blue waters. The slabs of the mountainsides reach into the dark sky, forming with the ruffled

13

surface of the lake a kind of tunnel through which we must travel.

We are all thinking of that June day in 1898 when the ice broke and that strangest of all armadas set off down this same corridor. The sun was shining and the prospectors in the boats were singing with joy to be moving at last after the long winter of packing and boat building. What a sight it must have been! Round boats and square boats, tiny canoes, huge scows—everything from catamarans to kayaks, heavily loaded as we are loaded, and drifting before the breeze past these shores. Twenty thousand men moving north; hundreds of shacks, cabins, tents and warehouses speckling these hillsides; and the smell of sawdust everywhere. No film can ever reproduce that spectacle. No one is alive today who remembers it and all we have are a few photographs and the written descriptions of those who were there. In a few hours it was over. The great wave of boats became a trickle. And in the intervening years nature has retrieved her lake: the hills, once stripped of timber by the boat builders, are wooded again; except for the station and the log church, the shores are empty. In the new growth, if you search diligently, you can find a few relics of the goldrush. Below the church there are stone foundations and back in the woods, poking up through a carpet of kinni-kinnick, the whitened bones of scores of cattle, butchered here and sold to the goldseekers; and beside the rapids that connect Lake Lindeman with Lake Bennett a gravestone with the name of Matthews still discernible—that same Tom Matthews who, after twice losing everything in those foaming waters, shot himself in despair.

Behind us, the little church grows smaller and disappears as we round a corner. The rain lessens and then ceases. Patches of blue appear between the clouds. We have come about as far as we expected on this first, short day and Skip is keeping his eyes open for a campsite. About fifteen miles down the lake he spots it – an abandoned sawmill on a small promontory, dwarfed by the rugged mountains.

How odd, I think, that the Yukon, historically the youngest part of Canada, should have become so quickly a land of artifacts. Rusting wheels, crumbling cabins, old roads blurred by new growth, the rotting carcasses of dredges and steamboats, gravestones, crosses, abandoned villages, ruined roadhouses – all this paraphernalia of the past is to be found strewn along the water highway between Lake Bennett and Dawson. We eat our minute steaks surrounded by broken machinery – cogs, gears, axles and flywheels half covered by shattered timbers, and, of course, the inevitable refuse of the Yukon: the mounds of glass telegraph insulators and ancient tin cans strewn through the bush. Sometimes I think the Yukon must be paved with tin cans. In my boyhood I remember roaming the hills above Dawson and seeing the tin cans, brown with age, forming a kind of mattress under the mosses and sedges. Great caches of tin cans could be found behind every cabin and even where the cabins had rotted away, these troves of old tins marked spots where men had once lived and worked. There were hundreds of cabins and thus hundreds of thousands of tin cans – bully beef, creamed corn, butter, devilled ham, lard, tomatoes, beans, beans, beans, preserved fruit, soup. Without the invention of the canning process, the Yukon could never have been settled.

The land, at first glance, seems untouched. The forests roll back endlessly from the lakeshore or rise sheer from the riverside, looking as they must have looked centuries ago, unmarked by saw or hatchet. But once you step out and move back into the tangle of bush, there are the tin cans, crumbling to rust and dust, slowly returning to the redden-

15

ing earth. Sometimes you can see the ghost of a label, even on the oldest tins, seared into the oxidizing metal. On the Chilkoot Pass the previous year I picked up a lard pail so old that it crumbled between my fingers, but I could still read the block letters on its surface: SWIFT's. It had lain there, just above that gravel ledge known as The Scales (where the way became so steep that the packers weighed every ounce and charged accordingly) for more than seventy years. An unspoken question formed in my mind: *Could this have belonged to my father?*

For he had come that way, climbing over those very rocks and resting at the summit, as we did, to gaze back down through the mists towards the seacoast. It was weird, as Peter put it, to think about that. Peter was with me on that Chilkoot trip, a boy just turned 16, and so was Pamela, who was 20, and it was during that brief, exacting journey that we first discussed taking the entire family down the river the following year. Skip, who was the outfitter for the Chilkoot party, encouraged the idea: "Listen," he said. "If you bring your family I'll handle your tour personal. Man, you couldn't *keep* me away!"

That decided it. It would be a journey through time as well as through space, even more than the Chilkoot had been. On the Chilkoot one was always conscious of time because the trail was thick with memories of the past: old shoes, broken sleds, rotting harness, the bones of horses, the skeletons of boats, bits and pieces of clothing, rusting cable, discarded pack sacks, barrels, pails, pots and pans, and, of course, tin cans. But the Chilkoot was for me, as it was for my children, a new experience. I had never crossed it before and so my only companions from the past were the ghosts of the stampeders whose mark was everywhere. But the Yukon was the river of my childhood and of my youth—as familiar, almost, as the streets of my home town; and so a voyage down the river with my family would be more than a voyage into history: it would be a journey into my own past. I had first come down the river in a small poling boat at the age of six with my father, my mother and my younger sister. I had last come up it at the age of 19, on a sternwheel steamboat, when my father was nearing the end of his days. In between I had travelled it from Whitehorse to Dawson at least half a dozen times. On the Chilkoot trail, more than thirty years after that last river trip, standing on the summit of the famous Pass, and thinking back to the moment when my father had stood there, I felt a yearning to experience the river once again. Service, who caught the spirit of the Yukon better than any writer, called it a land that "beckons and beckons." Dawson City, when I flew there in 1948 after a ten years' absence, looked so old and sad that I did not want to go back again. But I did go back in 1962 for the Goldrush Festival and in the summer of 1971, standing on the very lip of the divide that marks the Alaska-Yukon border, I felt the old pull.

My father stood there, at the Chilkoot's summit, on June 22, 1898, and scribbled part of a letter in pencil to his mother in Saint John. He had been counting the carcasses of horses that lay on the route between Sheep Camp and The Scales and he had counted no fewer than 38, ten of them in one heap. The main rush had gone by a month before, but my father's party was late because it had lost time trying to take the Stikine river route to the goldfields. It was an abortive trip, yet there is no sense of disappointment or frustration in my father's letters, only wonder and curiosity. His party had been marooned for two and a half days in a sandstorm on the Stikine, a storm that ruined much of their fresh food. They had struggled on upriver, towing their boat along the edge of the ice and meeting with the inevitable accidents along the way. ("It gave way under me once and I went in up to the hips but as the ice looked very shaky I had taken the precaution to take one of the poles with me and dropped on it. I got out in a hurry and crawled on hands and knees away from the bad spot. . . . We had pretty hard tugging and awfully slow progress from this on. . . .")

As it turned out, all this toil was in vain because the country north of Glenora was a heaving swamp and the packers wanted eight hundred dollars a ton to move goods to Teslin lake at the head of the Yukon. None of them could afford that and so they had to choose between backpacking the whole way – a delay of two months – or attempting the Chilkoot. One of the party was sent back to the seacoast to assess the possibilities of the Pass, where an overhead tramway was said to be in full operation. While waiting for his return, my father tramped the hills between Glenora and Telegraph creek, noting all manner of odd things – a species of western toad breeding in the pond and sending out spawn in long strings, flowers in wild profusion, many of which he was able to identify by their Latin names: a new species of ranunculus and of lobelia at six hundred feet, false Solomon Seal, a columbine with orange-red flowers that was new to him, monkshood and blue lupins of the kind he had grown himself, "a stonecrop very like the one you call Love-in-a-Tangle," and several varieties of orchids, which he carefully pressed and enclosed in his letters to his mother together with samples of the enormous northern mosquitoes (also pressed) and a detailed description of the uniforms of the North West Mounted Police, of whom he had read, but had never seen. When he reached Telegraph creek, my father hitched a ride back to Glenora by steamboat, paying for his passage by stoking coal. By that time his party had decided to attempt the Chilkoot. They bought a Peterborough canoe for twenty-seven dollars, added it to their several tons of supplies, and retraced their steps. At the summit of the Pass, when he next wrote his mother, they were all engaged in the arduous task of sledding their equipment in stages down the long mountain slopes towards the lakes. It took them a week to move everything to Mud lake, where the snow ended. Here, where firewood was so scarce that a few sticks cost three dollars (the price in those days of a tailor-made suit) they hired horses to move their supplies to Bennett and here, for one hundred dollars, they had to buy a second boat.

Late on July 2 he and his New Brunswick partners sailed their two craft with all their possessions down this same lake and past this very spot at which we are camped. For all we know they may well have stopped here: his diary records that they made fifteen miles that first evening and this is a logical camping place – the ground dark with the remnants of many fires. We sit around our own embers, the adults drinking rum out of coffee mugs, speculating on all this. Today is the birthday of two of the children: Penny, who has turned 24, and Paul, who has turned 14. The date is August 5, 1972 – almost another anniversary because it was on August 4, 1898 that my father reached Dawson, "the miners' mecca" as he called it in a letter home.

Peter's question comes back to me: Did he ever think his grandchildren would follow after him, seventy-four years later?

I doubt that he did, for he had no wife at the time, no prospects, no money and no plans to make the Yukon his home. But I cannot help wondering if his grandchildren will someday bring their own children down the river, on some future journey into time and space.

DAY TWO

Patsie has been assigned the task of keeping the log, partly because she is an uninhibited writer with an original though gaudy turn of phrase, partly because she is studying art and can illustrate her account of the river journey, and partly because she usually finishes any job she undertakes. On this Sunday morning, with the sun filtering through the clouds and the mountains around us still half-clothed in mist, she sits cross-legged on the bank with the logbook resting on her blue jeans. She is 19, but with her pixie face and puckish grin and darting black eyes she looks younger.

Patsie's features are rarely in repose but now as she concentrates on the log, the impish look is replaced by something else, hauntingly familiar. Where have I seen it before? In an old photograph album? When the hair is swept back, as it is now, and the grin vanishes, I suddenly see my mother reflected in Patsie's face – not the grand old lady, stiff-backed and white-haired, whom the children called "grandmamma" – but the girl of earlier photographs, so solemn with those immense black eyes and so lovely, with the jet hair pulled back in a tight coil to complete the perfect oval of the face. Patsie's hair is light brown and she has freckles and a snub nose, but the resemblance is there for a fleeting instant . . . uncanny . . . almost as if my mother's youthful ghost had entered her. This was how she must have looked to my father when, twelve years after he climbed the Chilkoot, he first met her at a party at Granville, the mining camp on the Indian river. He had already turned forty and was a thoroughgoing bachelor, but in a year or so all that was to change and, looking now at Patsie, I can see how beautiful my mother must have been to him. Then Patsie looks up from her logbook, her nose wrinkles, the familiar grin lights up her features, the black eyes come alive and the face in the photograph album disappears.

In the log, Patsie is describing Skagway, which we had left the previous morning on our journey through the White Pass to Bennett: "The sidewalks on the main street were all board and every building was like Shaw's old hardware [in Kleinburg]. It was a neat old place; many a derelict building with broken window or boarded-up door stood majestically – reminiscent of the glory they used to hold. I walked a while through the streets that were deserted – the wind blowing and whistling through my hair . . . a hollow building, a cracked window spied me from above . . . the wild grasses and flowers and weeds inhabited the streets where was once the adventure and splendour of the rough souls who stayed here. . . ."

We are slow getting ready this morning. Tents have to be taken down, dunnage bags packed, sleeping bags rolled, breakfast dishes washed, garbage buried, latrines filled in and all the baggage and provisions re-packed in the boats. We all don our rain gear: the lake is choppy this morning and when we enter the next lake, Tagish, we expect to face heavy weather. The boats are so heavily loaded that they cannot ride high in the water and even the smaller waves often break over the bows.

I catch young Paul lugging his dunnage bag down to the boats. This is strictly against doctor's orders and he knows it.

It is hard to realize that less than six weeks ago, Paul underwent heart surgery in the Sick Children's Hospital, Toronto. Nobody, I think, expected that he would make this trip, especially the members of the surgical team who worked over him for several hours late in June. Nobody except Paul. This family excursion probably means more to him than to anybody else except me because he has reached an age when the presence of the family has become important to him. The time will come in his later teens when the family may become too oppressive and he will want to escape for a while, but this year he is more insistent than any of the others on family outings and family rituals; Sunday dinners and summer picnics have become a passion with him. "The family is breaking up," he keeps saying sadly, for the children are growing older. This will probably be the last time our family finds itself together for a whole fortnight and this, too, has been one of the reasons for our river journey. On the Yukon, no one can intrude upon us; no one can reach us by wire, telephone or mail. We may drift for days without encountering another human being. We will be alone on the water and in the wilderness with each other's company and for Paul, especially, this is important.

It was late in June – the plans all made, the outfitter contracted for, the travel arrangements completed, the food shipped north – when Paul realized something was wrong. His heart felt funny, he said; within a week, for the second time in his life, he was on the operating table.

The doctor told us before the operation that he did not believe Paul could make the river trip. Any surgery required a convalescent period of eight weeks and this wasn't just any surgery. This was one of the most difficult of all operations, exhausting for the doctors as well as for the patient. The suggestion that he be taken almost directly from the hospital to a rubber raft and sent plunging down the wild Yukon was unthinkable. But the doctor reckoned without Paul.

He is the competitive member of the family, a boy who plays to win. He has a passion for games like *Risk, Careers* or *Monopoly*. There is a stubborn streak in him which makes him want to finish things he has started, no matter what the obstacles may be. The statistics of the Klondike stampede suggest that for every twenty men who decided to set out for the goldfields, only one actually made it. Paul would have been one of those who would make it, as my father was. My mother told me once that my father, thwarted on the Stikine and ready to attack the Chilkoot, was offered a chance to give up the struggle and return to a job he had long desired – a faculty post at Queen's University. The letter accepting his application was waiting for him at the Dyea post office before he scaled the Pass. It was a job for which he was perfectly suited, because he was a natural teacher; you could not talk to him for five minutes without learning something. Probably he should have taken the post and no doubt life would have been a great deal easier for him if he had. (He drifted about the Yukon for a dozen years, trying his hand at all sorts of odd employments; he was, by turn, carpenter, cook, miner, pick and shovel man, high school principal, and French instructor before he took a job with the government service.) But he had gone too far to turn back and so he put the letter in his pocket, forgot about it, climbed his Chilkoot and thus, by a conscious decision, changed the pattern of his life. Paul has some of his qualities. He literally willed himself better and was discharged a week ahead of schedule.

Some of our medical friends were horrified at the idea of Paul making the trip. What if his boat overturned? The shock could kill him. It was useless to explain that the healthiest of us would probably not survive if that happened. It is not just the numbing cold that makes a swim of any length impossible; it is also the current and the undertow. A stick flung in the water is sucked out of sight in an instant. We all faced an equal hazard.

But I wanted Paul to go and go he did with his own doctor's blessing. Keep him warm, he told us. Don't let him get wet or cold. And don't let him carry any heavy loads. So I warn Paul again, and he drops the bag and lopes off, muttering to himself. He is a boy who seems to find it impossible to walk anywhere.

It is a two-hour run under power to Carcross, the old Indian settlement on the spit of land that separates Bennett from Tagish lake. Already the three boats, with their twenty-five horsepower engines, have taken on personalities. Skip has names for them all. His is the fastest, named for a champion, *Miss Bardahl*. Cheri runs *The Sluice Box*, which the children have named *The Slush Box*. Each of these boats is fourteen feet long. The third is sixteen feet long and is called *The Pig*, and because it is much slower has already become an object of derision. Indeed, those who ride in The Pig are already being treated by the others as if they were members of an inferior social class. The loading of the boats then becomes a matter of more than logistics. Nobody wants to ride in The Pig, but each must take his turn. Every possible excuse to evade the draft is invented by those selected for The Pig. Since the boats must be equally balanced and since the weights of the passengers range from sixty to two hundred and twenty pounds and since certain people want to sit with certain other people, the arrangement in the boats requires the wisdom of a Solomon and the calculating powers of a small computer.

At last the cries of the enraged passengers in The Pig are

stilled and we set off down the choppy lake, the bottom of each boat slapping hard against the waves. The Pig's motor keeps sputtering and failing. The other boats are forced to slow down and there are jeers from the non-Piggers and wails from the Piggers and threats by me to put the jeerers into The Pig if they continue their abuse. The Pig has definitely become a boat to which one is condemned rather than assigned. When we reach Carcross in the early afternoon it is still bringing up the rear.

It is here that the great herds of caribou once crossed between the lakes. In my boyhood, the fall migration used to take place within a few miles of Dawson, never following the exact pathway two years in a row, but always leaving behind a trampled swath, almost as if a steamroller had pushed its way through the forest. My father would take us out on the river in his boat and we would watch the caribou thundering out of the woods, clambering down the banks, plunging into the river and swimming to the far side. Sometimes he would steer the boat into the midst of them and sometimes, when we had visitors with us, he would station them on an island and then, using his boat as a cowboy uses a horse, round up a swimming band and drive them past the gaping guests. Then we would watch as the animals reached the far side, the does getting behind the fawns and pushing them up the slippery bank with their noses. Not all of them made it. One of the keenest memories of my childhood is the sweet, not entirely unpleasant stench of rotting carcasses that hung over the river in the early fall. But all that has changed. There are still caribou roaming the forests of the Yukon, but the great herds are gone and the animals no longer cross between the lakes at Caribou Crossing.

Johnny Johns greets us from the wharf as Miss Bardahl noses in. He is a Tagish Indian who has lived with history—

born in the year of the goldrush, his kinfolk packers on the Chilkoot Trail. Johnny knew all the key figures in the stampede; George Carmack, who found the gold on Bonanza creek, a former packer, married to a Tagish Indian; Jim Mason, his brother-in-law, known as Skookum Jim because of the immense loads he carried over the Pass; another relative, Tagish Charley, who also took part in the famous discovery; and Kate Carmack, the wife Carmack deserted after he struck it rich. All except Carmack are buried here at Carcross and Johnny Johns tells us about the day when Tagish Charley got drunk and fell off the bridge here and was drowned in the lake, a victim of his own success because, being treated as a white man, he was allowed to drink in public. As for Johnny, he raises packhorses and makes a good living from it; at seventy-four he looks twenty years younger and it is clear that he will not fall off any bridges.

We are standing talking to Johnny in the shadow of the old *Tutshi*, the sternwheel steamer that once took tourists down the lake to a little settlement with the haunting name of Ben-My-Chree. In its day, Ben-My-Chree was known as the prettiest spot in the Yukon, for the soil was rich and the flower gardens there became the talk of the Territory. But now Ben-My-Chree, like most other settlements, is deserted and the *Tutshi* sits on the beach in relatively good condition and under the protection of the Territorial Government, her paint still gleaming white, her smoke-stack bright yellow, her paddlewheel the traditional scarlet, her pilot-house outlined in the familiar fretwork—a memorial to another time before the automobile and the airplane changed the pattern of travel in the North.

"Hey, you hear about Ben-My-Chree?" Johnny asks.

"What about Ben-My-Chree?"

"Some fella from the Outside bought it up."

"Bought it? All of it?"

"Whole place. Big wheel in the tourist business in Vancouver, so I hear."

"What for?"

"I don't know for sure. Maybe for tourist resort. He was up this way years ago, I hear tell. Maybe for sentimental reasons."

"Maybe he'll put the old *Tutshi* back into the water."

"Maybe. Be nice."

"Hey – that's *neat*," says Patsie.

"It's only neat if he fixed it up like it was before – or leaves it alone," says Pamela. "If he louses it up with hot dog stands or chicken stands, then it won't be so neat."

We stroll up to Matthew Watson's store to pick up a few provisions and I walk across to his home and talk to his mother, who knew my family in Dawson, where her father was the fire marshal. I remember him well, a sturdy man who wore a big fireman's hat and was the envy of every boy in school. I remember the firehall, and his men sliding down the pole when the siren sounded and the harness automatically dropped onto the horses. And I can remember the steam pumper, shining in the sun, full of chemical foam, rattling down the streets, pulled by the snorting animals. Steam pumpers were obsolete almost everywhere in Canada in those days except in Dawson. We used to buy a chocolate marshmallow bar called *Jus' Kids*, I remember, from which you could collect a set of cards about the Good Old Days, drawn by Jimmy Frise. One of these cards contained a drawing of a steam pumper, just like the one in Dawson, pulled by a spanking team of white horses and I could not for the life of me understand why such a commonplace spectacle should be included as part of the Good Old Days, which were, presumably, long past.

I say goodbye to Mrs. Watson, and join the children who have, as Patsie writes in the log, "gone to the pub to see the decrepit, swearing parrot." The parrot is very old; he was old in 1898 when he was brought here, which means he is probably twice as old as Johnny Johns. He is also very famous – so famous that when he dies, as he will in a few months, Canadian Press will carry his obituary. He is too decrepit to swear at us this morning, so, after buying a case of Yukon beer, we leave him and head for the boats.

"Watch out for Windy Arm," Johnny warns us, as we move down to the dock. "It can be very bad. But then you got good boats for it."

The Windy Arm of Tagish lake, an unprotected and shallow stretch of water that cannot be avoided, is known as the roughest in all the Yukon. Here the waves can reach five feet in height. In the goldrush days, this was many a prospector's finish. One can imagine that ill-assorted fleet of small craft, strung out at this point for the entire length of two lakes, facing those mountainous swells. Those who were wise waited for the wind to die; those who were greedy for the Klondike's gold went on to be drenched or swamped and sometimes drowned in their ungainly floating coffins.

Skip has laid his plans for Windy Arm. We must lighten our boats before we face those waves so we remove from The Pig all the provisions that we will not need over the next two days. These will be shipped by train to Whitehorse and Scotty Jeffers will go ahead with them and pick up a suitable freight canoe. This accomplished, we wave goodbye to Johnny Johns and set out down the mountain-ringed expanse of Tagish lake, in the face of a stiff breeze. We can guess what Windy Arm is going to be like.

Peggy Anne, who is 11, says she doesn't like the colour of the water – a dark, almost navy blue. When the sun is shining and the air is calm, these mountain lakes change to a soft green, almost exactly the colour of the larch in the early spring; but when the weather grows angry, the lakes darken and seem to frown. Peggy Anne is an imaginative child, fearful of nameless things that lurk in the gloomy forests and dark corners. When she travels she expects that airplanes will crash and ships will founder and I can sympathize with her, for I believed exactly the same thing when I was her age. I still remember the terror of my first trip to the Outside, as Northerners call the rest of the world. I was five years old but not too young to pray and after we left Skagway I prayed every night that the s. s. *Princess Louise* would not sink. I had some reason for apprehension because the *Louise's* sister ship, *Princess Sophia*, had done just that in 1919, slipping off a rock and sinking with every soul on board, a disaster that affected almost every family in Dawson. When the *Sophia* was mentioned, a kind of shiver went through the room, and this was not lost on a small, apprehensive boy. Nor did it escape me or anyone else that the CPR changed its schedule so that the Alaskan vessels always passed the scene of that tragedy at night – a piece of useless camouflage that only heightened the horror.

Peggy Anne, and her younger sister, Perri, who is 7, are with me in Miss Bardahl, along with Skip and Paul, who sits beside me, warmly bundled. We are wearing rain gear with the hoods up and the pants and jackets tightly tied. Ahead of us, we can see for the first time rows of whitecaps against the dark waters. Windy Arm is indeed windy and this crossing is going to be one to remember.

An hour later we are into it. The boat hits each oncoming wave with a hard smack, bounces high and smacks again. If Peggy Anne is frightened, she does not show it; indeed, she is laughing at the bumps, while her little sister is positively gleeful. It occurs to me that for them it is rather like a ride in an amusement park.

We turn to the rear so that we can take the waves on our backs. Only Skip Burns, steering the boat, must face into the storm. With each smack, the bow dips under the water and a four-foot wave rolls over us. Even with our rain gear tied tightly, the water manages to trickle inside our necks and shoes. Each wave catches Skip full in the face. His shock of red hair and drooping mustache are soaking wet but he manages to keep his eye on the far shore. An ordinary boat would be half full of water by now but these inflated craft are designed to be self-flushing. Skip pulls out a plug in the stern and the forward movement forces the bilge water out.

The waves increase in fury. The boat pitches crazily. I try to look back through the binoculars but it is impossible. Well behind us I can occasionally glimpse The Slush Box. She seems to be dipping directly into the water, like a submarine, only to rise and then dip again. Of the slower Pig there is no sign.

So it goes for forty-five minutes until we reach a small wooded island and, for the moment, the ordeal is over.

"We're about at the half-way point," Skip says. "Might as well have some lunch before we go at her again."

We have stripped off our rain gear and have a fire going by the time The Slush Box arrives. Behind it, rolling like a fat log and labouring in the heavy swell, we can spot The Pig almost enveloped in foam. The passengers in the other boats are wetter than we are. Patsie has already stripped down to her long underwear and, with the others, is huddling over the fire. She has opened up her dripping pack and laid out all her clothes to dry on nearby bushes. Fortunately the sun has come out and the fire is a good one. We cook hot dogs on long sticks and drink the whole case of beer. As Patsie puts it, in the log, "it was quite bliss after having our mandatory bath." As for the journey across Windy Arm "although it was dangerous and scary it was fun and adventurous and gave us something to talk about."

But the journey is only half over. Two hours later, damp still but warmer, we face the whitecaps again and the ordeal is repeated for another forty-five minutes. At last we reach the lee of the shoreline and the waters grow calmer. Ahead of us lies Tagish Post in the channel that leads to Marsh lake. Here, in the stampede days, every boat was required to stop and check in with the Mounted Police. (My father stopped here and registered at 3 a.m. on July 4, 1898.) Now, like almost every settlement on the water route to Dawson, it has vanished.

We enter Marsh lake and, not far from Tagish Post, we make camp for the evening. The boats look as if a disaster has hit them, as indeed one has. Our nineteen cardboard boxes have been reduced to sodden mush. Fortunately much of the food has been packed in plastic but some is inedible: a tin box of Peek Frean's biscuits, though tightly sealed, is half full of water.

"Thank God for plastic garbage bags!" says Janet, whom Skip is already calling "Mama." She has had the good sense to line every cardboard box with one. "But why," she asks herself, "didn't I pack everything in wooden crates?" She and Pamela are now sorting out the mess and trying to mark the right days on the right bags.

Dinner is discovered in the remains of a box on which we can still see the faintly pencilled words DAY TWO. We will sit down to a meal of asparagus soup, sauerkraut, apple butter, smoked pork chops and fruit. Patsie, who is a vegetarian and has brought along supplies of her own, such as red lentils and crunchy Granola, welcomes this meal because she can enjoy all of it except the pork chops.

Most of the group retires early but one or two of us stay

31

up to catch the sun's glow reddening the blue hills and to listen to Skip Burns tell the story of his wedding day, just four days before – a wedding such as the North had never seen before. He tells it with great feeling in the soft North Carolina accent that Peggy Anne unconsciously imitates. ("Skip says it's tam to raz and shan," she told me the first morning. "What does 'tam to raz and shan' mean?")

"The idea first came to me after three years of hiking that Chilkoot Trail," Skip is saying. "We were originally going to have the ceremony at Crater lake, just below the summit, but the people, you know, decided it would be awful difficult getting away up there, so the second choice was the old log church at Bennett and it was a good one."

On the day of the wedding, one hundred and sixty-seven people turned up on the shores of Lake Bennett.

"You should have seen it," Skip said. "All colours of tents all over the hills. It was like the great tent city of '98 all over again."

The guests ranged all the way from Chilkoot packers to a long-haired rock group who brought along an organ, violin, flute and drums. I had heard about this band in the lunch-room at Bennett; by all accounts it never stopped playing. Two of Skip's great aunts came up from North Carolina and so did his 76-year-old grandmother, a member of the family he described as "in the final throes of southern aristocracy." The oldest guest was 82 and the youngest three.

To feed this army Skip supplied sixteen hams and as many turkeys, several wheels of Canadian and Swiss cheese, sixteen watermelons, two bushels of grapes, two more of apples, and a barrel each of pickles, pilot bread, peanuts and popcorn. There were also eighty cases of beer and the logistic and legal problems of getting *that* to Bennett would have defeated a less determined entrepreneur. Bennett has no beer store and, since it is in British Columbia, it is illegal to import cases from either Alaska or the Yukon Territory. Skip got on the phone to the Liquor Control Boards in Victoria and Whitehorse and in the end was granted a special permit. "It's never been done before," the man in B.C. told him, "but I'm not going to have this on my conscience."

Skip has all the eloquence of a true romantic and as he tells the story of the wonderful wedding, it comes alive for us: the tents billowing on the hillside above the lake, the picnic trestles loaded with food, the rock band in full throat and then the service itself in the early evening.

"That service was totally designed by Cheri and myself. The main part was the two of us telling the guests why we had chosen to become married. After that we had special music. One of our helpers, who's 15, played the first song on the organ and that was *The Impossible Dream*. The very last song was played by the whole rock group; it was a Cat Stevens song but I forget the name right now. Then after the music, the Unitarian minister made it all nice and legal."

As Skip talks, the pink in the sky is giving way to grey. Cheri sits next to her husband, nodding occasionally, but saying very little. Below us, the surface of the lake loses its glitter and changes to sheet metal. Behind us, a flashlight glimmers in the woods. There is no wind; even the aspen leaves have stopped trembling. The hills go from blue to black as dusk falls.

"Let me tell you what Cheri wore," Skip says. "She wore this gown, which was an 1898 gown. Ruffles all the way down, you know? The most beautiful wedding dress I've ever seen. Well, I had for me some special pants made. They were blue suede. And I had a wedding shirt made to my own design but patterned roughly after an 1898 shirt. We played some roles that day, I can tell you."

I remember them as I first saw them in their tattered blue jeans, bent double under the weight of their packs and struggling up the forty-five degree incline of the Chilkoot. As Skip talks, I see them again, in that oddly effective Victorian garb, standing before their congregation of friends and explaining why they had decided to marry. Everyone was standing up for that service because the Bennett church has no pews. But Skip's friends had cleaned it from tower to nave, spread a carpet of evergreen boughs on the dirt floor and built an altar out of rocks, decorated with wild flowers and 104 specially-made candles. The church has no windows but the work party had made one from broken bottles – worn pieces of coloured glass that had lain hidden in the sedges since the goldrush days and which now spelled out the word PEACE above the altar.

"Cheri and I were to sleep in the steeple of the church. There's no floor there, either, but somebody picked up all the boards they could find in Bennett and made one. You know, it was just an incredible evening. The church and the whole area around was full of some kind of energy. It was love all around." He puts his arm around his young bride and she lays her head on his shoulder. We can no longer see the far hills. It must be close to midnight.

I had heard that it poured rain all night but Skip tells us that this in no way dampened the spirits of the wedding party. The following day everybody packed up and tried to get on the train to Skagway. By some misfortune the reservations had been ignored and, as the train was oversold, there were no seats left.

"What did you do, Skip?"

"They were very good about it, the train people. They just kind of broke the rules and let everybody ride back."

I had heard about the ride, which must have been a

34

memorable one: one hundred and sixty-seven people, soaking wet, standing all the way and singing their heads off to the music of the organ. The tourists who came to visit the peaceful Yukon must have been baffled.

"Well," Skip says, "there were some who were just a bit overwhelmed, yes."

"What about your grandmother and those two great aunts from North Carolina? How did they take it?"

"Well, sir, that was probably the tensest part of the whole thing. I was really apprehensive, you know, about what they might think of that wedding, particularly the great aunts that I hardly knew anyway. But it was a good thing for them because they all left with smiles on. And one of my great aunts at the wedding, well it took me half an hour to get her to stop crying, even when it was over.

"Come to that," Skip says, "I was pretty choked up myself."

DAY THREE

We are not yet an organized camping party; merely a cheerful rabble. It is eleven before we push off down Marsh lake and Skip says it will help if we can cut an hour off our departure time. Yet this is, after all, a holiday and nobody wants to be part of a military operation. "Stop cracking the whip, Dad," says Penny, when I try to hurry everybody along. I swallow my retort. "You're so much alike, you two," Janet reminds me. "You strike sparks off each other. You can't push Penny." You can't push her sister, Pamela, either but for totally different reasons. How is it, I often wonder, that two daughters born of the same parents within eighteen months can be so different? "Penny reminds me a lot of you when you can't find your socks," Janet says. I see myself, rushing about the house, screaming for my socks, and I have to laugh. If Pamela cannot find her socks—and there are days when she cannot seem to find anything—she merely goes barefoot. One is like the mother, the other like the father—even to the physical resemblance. But both have my own mother's large brown eyes, which she, in turn, inherited from her father.

Penny wants to be a film maker and she is making films now with our Super-8 as we set off down the lake. The morning is bright and the water is calm. All of these lakes are exquisite when the sun shines. The colours change constantly, from Nile green to deep purple and the surrounding hills change colour, too, depending on the mood of the weather. Today they are shadowy blue, blending imperceptibly with the frost blue of the sky. The occasional cloud scuds across the mountain tops, its shadow turning the slopes violet. The flanks of the mountains are scarred and pitted by glacial fans and spangled with the silver thread of cataracts that hang suspended from the upper ledges. Ahead of us, a flock of Merganser ducks scoots up from the water and settles again a hundred yards away. Little spotted sandpipers skitter along the banks. Sometimes in the sky we can see a kestrel wheeling and later on the occupants of The Pig gain status by spotting a bald eagle diving for a fish.

In time we reach the end of Marsh lake and there, ahead of me, I see the first familiar hills bordering the Yukon river proper—hills that are for me like no other hills, their shoulders dark with spruce, their rounded tops bare of trees and grooved by time. Directly ahead lies Miles Canyon, the once-dreaded gorge which Lieut. Frederick Schwatka, the explorer, named after his boss, General Miles of the United States Army. Schwatka also named Lake Bennett after the publisher of the New York *Herald*. In fact, he named every major point on the river so that today a good many familiar names in the Canadian Yukon are American; but then it was a United States cavalry officer, not a Canadian, who first thought to follow the great river from its source to its mouth.

We turn our motors off and plan to paddle through the canyon while Penny's friend, Robert Holmes, leaps off onto the shore to photograph the adventure. There was a time when this journey through the gorge and the rapids beyond was considered a dangerous feat. In the first days of the stampede scores of boats were wrecked here; outfits were ruined and several lives lost. But a power dam at the far end has tamed the canyon so that it is now no more than a carnival ride.

My father reached the canyon on July 7, 1898, and promptly sent a postcard to his mother: "We have now passed one of the greatest obstacles in our journey, the White Horse rapids, which we did not attempt to shoot. We had the stuff packed on the tramway from the canoe, and the canoe as well, and part of the stuff from the boat. A pilot took charge of the boat through the Canyon and Rapids with Charlie and Mart in it. It must have been very exciting. The rest of us walked. The tramway (there are 2, one on each side of the canyon) is about 3 miles long with wooden rails, squared on the one we came by & round logs on the other. Canyon is 3 miles long, 9 mile current & 60 ft. wide with cliffs of columnar basalt, probably like Giant's Causeway in Ireland . . . 30 or 40 feet high & perpendicular. Current in rapids 15 miles an hr. A boat went up yesterday with 1st consignment of gold from Dawson. Reports vary from ½ to 2 million. The owners were pitching horseshoes at $100 a shot. (Not a game, mark you, but a shot!) Mosquitoes frightfully thick & vicious. Love, Frank."

The red basalt walls rise above us as we slide into the canyon. My father underestimated their height; actually they rise for seventy-five feet. In the centre, the canyon widens out and here, in the old days, the stampeders encountered a great whirlpool that sucked more than one boat under. It is scarcely visible now in the higher water caused by the dam.

Above us people are standing on the bridge across the canyon, waving to us; our passage, seen from above, looks far more hazardous than it really is—or so Robert tells me. I can see him, on the bridge, focussing his camera. With his blonde beard and long hair he looks a bit like General Custer.

On the far side of the canyon, we can see the power dam

which has obliterated the famous rapids from which the town of Whitehorse takes its name. The Yukon river runs for 2200 miles from Lake Bennett to the Bering Sea, navigable for its entire distance, and the dam is the only obstacle in all that distance. The power interests have for years looked at this wild river with hungry eyes. There is an immediate four millions of horsepower to be harnessed here and an ultimate twelve millions or more. There have been plans on both sides of the border for a series of dams on the Yukon – projects I find truly horrifying. One scheme is to dam the river below Whitehorse and then turn it back upon itself so it flows towards the Alaskan coast. This would involve flooding the beautiful land through which we have just come. The sinuous lakes would become bloated. Every trace of the goldrush would be obliterated. The river would be forced back through tunnels in the Coastal Mountains into penstocks on the Alaskan side. The results would be similar to those caused by the Kitimat power development in British Columbia. That project destroyed half of Tweedsmuir National Park. I have seen the destruction from the air: each swollen lake is encircled by a ring of broken trees and rotting vegetation several hundred yards deep – a labyrinth of dead-falls, drowned in the rising waters, so impenetrable that the moose and other game can no longer make their way to the water's edge to feed. No energy crisis in the world is worth this obscenity but there are still those who talk glibly of the Yukon's great potential. The potential is there – but not in horsepower. The potential is the river itself, unchanged and unchanging, coiling majestically through the whole of the Yukon and Alaska, past unscarred forests to its rendezvous with the sea.

We pull the boats into the shores of the man-made lake, named for Lieut. Schwatka. Trucks will move everything around the dam site. Meanwhile, Janet will forage for new food cartons and extra supplies–especially rubber boots– while the rest of us look over Whitehorse.

It is not the most prepossessing community in Canada. Patsie describes it as "a minute cosmopolitan blight upon the rich land of stark rock and evergreen mountain." I was born here but my parents moved back to Dawson when I was still a baby. I cannot even find the house in which I was first raised, though I know it still exists. My memories of White-horse go back to the fall of 1939, when it was a sleepy hamlet of three hundred people nestled on a strip of volcanic soil between the benchland and the river. There was scarcely any traffic on the dusty roads. The biggest event of the day was the arrival of the train from Skagway. But on that day in 1939 there was more important news: war had been declared in Europe, a catastrophe that would transform Whitehorse. When I next saw the town, it had become the anchor point for the Alaska Highway and the North West staging route– and was almost unrecognizable. Today, except for the old steamboats, a few log cabins and some relics in the goldrush museum, Whitehorse is like any other small, badly developed Canadian town of twelve thousand. We drive out to the Takhini Hot Springs through the inevitable strip develop-ment–chicken palaces, car lots, motels and drive-ins–and we might be anywhere: Brampton or Calgary or Victoria. Only the green river, rustling past the town on its long journey to the sea, makes Whitehorse special.

At Takhini we shower away the Yukon's grime and then sit and relax up to our necks in the steaming water. The small children splash about in the shallow concrete pool and giggle with delight; the rest of us just soak. There are hot springs to be found all through the so-called Frozen North, from the top of British Columbia to the heart of Alaska.

The finest of all are on the Liard river. There, the wild violets, grown fat as pansies in the steam, are bunched right to the water's edge and the pools have been left in their natural state.

"Remember last year, eh Dad?" Peter reminds me. "How good it felt?" We had come down from the Chilkoot and picked up the Whitehorse train at Bennett and gone directly to these hot springs, every muscle aching from our long climb over the Pass. These therapeutic sulphur waters were exactly what we needed.

We soak for an hour, dress and return by car to the boats, which are moored downstream hard by the old shipyard, in the very shadow of the decaying sternwheeler, *Whitehorse*, which towers above us, her white paint long faded but her name still visible on the pilot-house. On the other side of town, they have restored the *Klondike*, the last steamboat ever built on the river, but it is really the *Whitehorse* that should be kept as a reminder of the steamboat days. All her sister craft foundered. The *Dawson* sank in Rink Rapids in 1925. The *Casca* struck the Dawson's hull a few years later and was abandoned. The original *Klondike* sank in the Thirtymile. The *Nasutlin* and the *Aksala* and the *Yukon* are all gone. But the *Whitehorse* continued in service to the end. Now this brave old steamer, which survived the rapids and the ice and the vagaries of the twisting channels, cannot retard the onset of old age any more than she could compete with the changing cycle of transportation. Like the old sourdoughs, who used to sit on the verandah of St. Mary's Hospital in Dawson, she is slowly fading away and will soon be gone.

I never think of the steamboat days without thinking of my friend Hambone. In Victoria, after we left the Yukon, he was my closest crony. We met in the Boy Scouts and each

41

became patrol leaders. We put out the troop newspaper together, helped plan the campfire entertainments and every Sunday, rain or shine, we took our patrols together on a hike, usually to Thetis lake, then a wooded area far from town. When the sun shone, the others came along; but when it rained Hambone and I would set off all alone, wearing our yellow slickers. It is those rainy days I remember best, the two of us trudging resolutely through the woods, with the water dripping off our broad Scout hats. It was a point of honour to cook a meal in the rain. Usually, we took shelter under a bridge, made a fire using the mandatory single match, fried up beans in a pan and talked about life and the future and our friends at school and the girls we were afraid to date.

When I was 17 I set off again for the Yukon to get a summer job in a mining camp. Nobody believed I could get a job because jobs were almost nonexistent in the 1930s. When I told my friends that jobs in the Yukon were paying the unbelievable sum of $4.50 a day, they refused to believe me. But with my father's help I got such a job and when I returned to Victoria in the fall I urged Hambone to come north with me the following year.

All that winter we made our plans. Then, in May, a few days before we were to leave, a telegram arrived from Dawson. Jobs had suddenly become scarce. Scores of unemployed men were roaming the streets. There would be a job for me but not for Hambone.

"Dammit," said Hambone, "I'm going anyway! I'll find something."

What he found was a job on a steamboat. He became a steward on the old *Keno* and though it didn't pay as well as the mining camp it was far pleasanter to spend the summer chugging up and down the river, than to work in ankle deep mud on the flats of Dominion creek. When we met again that fall Hambone had become a confirmed and enthusiastic Yukoner.

Our close comradeship ended about that time. University and the army separated us. In the thirty-odd years since, I have seen Hambone on only two occasions, both of them lamentably brief. He went into the tourist business for a while, I heard, but after that I lost track of him. Now, looking up at the splintered bulk of the old sternwheeler, I think of him again and wonder where he is and what he's doing.

We are not yet ready to leave. My nephew, Berton, who plans to become a journalist in the family tradition, is writing a series of articles about the trip, which he hopes will help him get his foot in the editorial door of a Vancouver newspaper. He is off interviewing Alan Innes-Taylor, the old Yukon hand who knows more about the river than anyone alive and who has provided us with a set of old steamboat charts for our journey. Some of us go off in search of Berton, stopping for a cold beer on the way.

It is easier to drink in the Yukon than anywhere else in Canada because of the new liquor laws. You can drink anything you want anywhere you want. You can drink in the middle of the street (as long as you don't impede traffic) and some, apparently, do. You can drink in your car, and some do that, too. You can drink while *driving* your car as long as you are not impaired. You can buy a case of beer in a tavern and cart it away with you. A bar can legally stay open all night, if it chooses, because there are no longer any restrictive drinking hours in the Territory. The laws were eased because those in charge decided the alcohol problem could not possibly be any worse than it was and because the Mounted Police were spending too much time dealing with simple liquor offenses. The rate of drunkenness in the Yukon, so I am told, is about the same–no more since the laws were altered (that was impossible) and probably no less. But the jails are no longer crowded.

We finish our beer and drop in to the tourist agency that Skip uses in Whitehorse. Berton isn't there but we chat a while about the tourist business, which is increasing. The Territory's most precious natural asset, it seems to me, is no longer gold, silver or base metals–though many Yukoners still cling to this idea. People in the urban south are hungering for the wilderness and the more they crowd into the cities the more they want to get away. Here, the wilderness rolls on, like the river, for hundreds of miles, scarred and blackened only where the mining interests have invaded the land and retreated. Anyone raised in a mining town knows to his sorrow what happens when the mines run out, as run out they must. How transitory is gold! Most of the Klondike's treasure, torn from the frozen bedrock, was shipped away by foreigners who mined it, profited from it and returned it to the earth again beneath Fort Knox, U.S.A. But when the tourists come, they bring gold with them and it stays in the country. The real problem is how to save the country for the visitors and at the same time save it *from* them. Too many newcomers could ravage the land as easily as the miners.

"Did you know somebody bought Ben-My-Chree?" I am asked.

"I heard about it at Carcross. Do you know who it was?"

"Sure. Fellow named Cy Porter. Used to be in the tourist business in Vancouver. Know him?"

Indeed, I do know him. His name, in my time, was Cyril Pridham, but he later took that of his foster parents who brought him up from childhood in one of the Gulf Islands.

So . . . the man who bought Ben-My-Chree was my old friend, Hambone! He, too, had never been able to get the Yukon out of his blood. Well, Ben-My-Chree would be in good hands.

When we return to the boats, we find Berton already there. He is not hard to spot in his crimson jacket and his father's old artillery hat. He has his mother's dark brown eyes – his grandmother's eyes – and he has his maternal great grandfather's instincts. Like him, he is a Marxist and like him, he is going to be a journalist. Looking at Berton, I think again of my mother's father whom I knew only briefly as a small visiting child, and of whom I was always a little afraid, although he was the gentlest of men. He was very old and almost blind but he worked every day at his desk, dictating his pieces to my mother's younger sister – a writer who could never stop writing. In the evenings he would sing the old songs: *The International* and *The Red Flag* and *Drill, Ye Tarriers, Drill* and many others, most of them political. It was in this atmosphere that my mother had been raised, a city atmosphere of intellectual and political discussion and much poverty. What a contrast it must have been for her when she stepped off the steamboat in 1908 and found herself in a Yukon mining camp. But she has already told that tale in a book of her own.

At last the boats are re-loaded and we are ready to leave. Scotty Jeffers has packed the big freight canoe with most of our provisions and we all sigh our relief, for that means there will be more room and the boats will ride higher when we reach Lake Laberge tomorrow.

An old Indian, who has been sitting in the shadow of the *Whitehorse*, gets to his feet and walks down to talk to us. He is a little drunk.

"Be careful of Lake Laberge," he says. "Be careful of sudden squalls."

The words are like an echo, ringing down the corridors of the decades. My mind goes back to a July day in 1926 and to this very spot in the lee of the old steamboats, rotting on the ways. (But the *Whitehorse*, bright with fresh paint, was then in the water.) Another boat loaded with provisions was tied to this bank, ready to push off down the river. It was called *The P and L* which stood for Pierre and Lucy. My father had named it for his children.

Down the bank to see us off came the Bishop of the Yukon, Isaac Stringer, dressed in traditional fashion, black gaiters and all. This was no comic bishop out of a Chaplin movie. This big man was as tough as a pilot biscuit – the same bishop who, starving on the Rat River Divide, had boiled and eaten his boots, thus saving his life. That, it is said, provided Chaplin with his most famous scene.

"Be careful of squalls on Lake Laberge," I can hear the bishop saying and I remember wondering to myself exactly what a squall was. Was it like a squaw? I had only turned six and did not know all the words yet.

"We'll watch out, Bishop," my father said.

"Keep close to the shore, Frank. If a squall comes up and you're out in the middle, you'll never make it. You know how fast they come up on Laberge."

"We're going to creep around the shore, Bishop," my father said. And then we got into the boat and waved good-bye to the Bishop Who Ate His Boots and went drifting with the current towards the lake.

Dusk is about to fall as our own rubber boats and freight canoe push off. We will not travel for long. But we want to get as far downstream from Whitehorse as possible, to escape the pollution it has brought to this section of the river. Raw sewage from the town pours directly into the Yukon and, as we round the corner, we see a mountain of steaming garbage clinging to the high bank and spilling into the water. The dump was not there when *The P and L* slipped down the river forty-six years ago and it was not there when the steamer *Whitehorse* brought me past these banks on the first day of a new war. If my children bring their children down the same river on some future odyssey, will the spreading chancre of civilization have turned the whole river into a sewer? Or will that generation, wiser than ours, find some way to preserve these waters for the children who follow?

DAY FOUR

I wake to the unwelcome sound of rain pelting against the nylon tent. We have forgotten to fasten the flap and the foot of my sleeping bag is soaking wet. It is well past seven but no one is stirring. Perri, I am sure, is awake for she is a morning person, chipper as a squirrel at the earliest hour. On this trip, she has usually been the first to rise, the first to dress and the first to pop out of her tent but there is no sign of her this morning.

Reluctantly, I pull on my clothes, rain gear and rubber boots and poke my head out. The forest is sopping. Pools of water drown the grasses under my feet as I slop over to the riverbank. Last night's campfire is a blackened mush. Many of the new cartons that Janet picked up in Whitehorse are already damp under sodden tarpaulins. We have two choices: we can stay huddled in the tents and wait out the rain or have a swift breakfast and push off toward the patch of open sky that lies in the direction of Lake Laberge. I choose the second course. We will try to outrun the rain.

I search about for a large tree, chip off the wet outer bark and make a fire out of the drier inner pieces, recalling the old days at Thetis lake with Hambone. This morning one match is not enough: it takes a tinful of gasoline to get a blaze going. My plan is to feed everybody in the tents, so that they can keep dry as long as possible. Last night we ate most of a fine country ham. Breakfast will be hot ham sandwiches and cocoa. Perri turns up, wearing her rain hat, plastic coat and rubber boots, and volunteers to help. Skip and his crew start to load the boats. When everybody is fed, the tents come down in a rush; then in a burst of energy we pack up and set off under full power, fleeing from the rain. By the time we reach Laberge we are out of it.

As we enter the mirror-smooth lake we can see the ruins of the old Mounted Police post on our left. The rain is following us, a dark smear against the forest, but here the waters are smiling in the sun. Around us, rocky cliffs and steep hills rise from the shoreline, and to the west and southeast we can see lines of snowcapped mountains, but as we move farther down the lake, the hills grow smaller. We scud across the glassy surface, each boat nicely trimmed and up on its step, like a seaplane's float. It will take us only a few hours to make the thirty-one mile run. It took *The P and L* the better part of a week.

The crossing of this lake and the sudden plunge through the Five Finger Rapids are the two memories that stand out from that childhood voyage. My father had made a sail for our boat but the wind did not rise and we had to cling to the shoreline while he rowed the full length of Laberge. The exercise did not bother him. He was 56 but as powerful as a grizzly and this was the first holiday he had taken since the end of the Great War. The previous winter had been a lonely one, for the rest of us had been Outside, visiting my mother's parents in Ontario. No doubt that was the reason he bought up the equipment of a departing dentist and began to fill and pull teeth: it was a way of putting in time. Where he learned the technique I do not know; perhaps he got it out of a book. At any rate, for several years after that my mouth was filled with plaster of Paris, as he experimented with making moulds for false teeth.

My father could not go East with us. As a government mining recorder he was given two weeks' holiday a year but in those days it took two weeks to reach Ontario. The Yukon was a kind of prison for men on salary. There were no airplanes; the first one did not reach Dawson until 1927. It took several days to reach Whitehorse by steamboat, another day by train to Skagway, then several more days down the coast to Vancouver and another four days by train to Toronto. In the winter, the only escape was by open sleigh – an exhausting five-day journey to Whitehorse in temperatures that often dropped to 40 below. Because of this, the government allowed its employees to accumulate their holidays over a period of years but my father had not yet saved up enough to make the Outside journey worthwhile. It would be another seven years before he was able to spend a full winter away from Dawson. For more than ten years he did not have a day off except for those three weeks on the river. He worked a five and one-half day week, week in and week out; when he met us in Whitehorse he had not seen us since the previous fall.

I do not think he minded not having holidays, since there were compensations. He walked home a block and a half for lunch. He was finished work at 4:30. He never experienced the tensions or frustrations of city life. He never needed a car. Living in Dawson during the short, intense summers was like living in a summer camp. In June, July and August, the river was his highway and the Klondike valley his fishing ground. The winters could be viciously cold but he made the most of them; it amused him to fashion a scarf pin out of mercury, which freezes at 40 below, and see how long it would last. And when he walked home from work in the pitch darkness, he could examine the stars, which were an eternal fascination to him. In the *Scientific American,* which he saved for winter reading and absorbed thoroughly, there were monthly maps of the heavens and these he committed to memory. He and I would study the star maps and he would teach me the names of the constellations of Orion and Andromeda and the Pleiades and the Little Bear and show me how to find the North Star by using the pointers of the Big Dipper. And then we would go out into the snow and gaze up into the night and pick out the pinpoints of the real stars, shining more brightly than they do in the cities because the air was free from smog and the stars were the only lights that shone around us.

More than most men today, my father had time for his family. Often on the way home from school, my sister and I would go into his office and wait for him to finish, watching him as he worked at his desk, the armlets keeping his cuffs high, a green eye-shade on his forehead. Then we would be allowed to ride on the carts as the great books of mining files were rolled back into the vault at closing time and we would take his hand and walk with him up the steep roadway that led to our home.

This river trip was one of the great events of his life. He rarely reminisced about the stampede; it was so much a part of the background of the town that it was taken for granted. But in the years that followed, he and my mother constantly looked back on those sunlit days when we rowed around Laberge and drifted down the river. My sister and I still talk about it whenever we meet. We were very young at the time; I had just turned six and she was not yet five, but certain moments of that journey are forever imprinted on our minds. *Remember how they took the bread to bed with them to make it rise? Remember how he scooped an oven out of the bank? Remember how we shot the rapids and Mamma wanted to get out? Remember the day on Lake Laberge when we caught the big fish?*

It all comes back again – that sudden tug on the rolling line. *It can't be a fish; you must have snagged the bottom . . . No, by George, it is a fish and it's a whopper . . . Damn, I've got no net . . . have to use a knife . . . Don't look, children . . .* My mother raised a large black umbrella and popped us beneath it, but I peeked out and in one forbidden instant witnessed a thrilling spectacle: a fish that seemed as big as a shark, lashing about in the boat, and my father, hunting knife in hand, standing astride the seat and stabbing it to death. It was big enough to serve us all for three full meals. There are fewer fish in Lake Laberge today; pollution from Whitehorse has taken its toll.

Now the present intrudes upon the past. When we are about two-thirds of the way down the lake the weather abruptly changes. The sun vanishes. A stiff wind springs out of nowhere. The waters turn choppy. A kind of darkness settles over Laberge.

The boats are strung out for about a mile. Far to the rear I can see The Pig making heavy weather, the rising waves already breaking across her bow. Scotty Jeffers, in the freight canoe, has been running beside us but now he drops back. Skip's lead boat still rides high, but as the going gets rougher and the waves higher, it becomes more difficult to manoeuvre. We feel a cold spray on our faces and then the spray grows heavier and buckets of water begin to wash over us. The wind continues to rise, the waves to heighten, and the boats are now slap-slapping against the hardness of the water, like wagons bumping over a rocky road. This is the dreaded Lake Laberge squall, which I have been hearing about since childhood but have never experienced. I remember the entry in my father's diary for July 9, 1898: "Bad wind across lake sprung up & we had hard time to make camping ground."

Peter, who loves engines, has been at the tiller with Skip beside him. Suddenly Skip's face changes. He seizes the tiller from Peter and swings the boat around. "Scotty's in trouble," he says.

As the boat turns, I look back and see the raised paddle that is our signal for distress. I feel a strange sensation in my stomach. The freight canoe, which holds all of our provisions and most of our kit and equipment, has fallen far behind and is clearly about to sink. Indeed, it appears to have gone under, for all we can see through the waves and the spray is the figure of Scotty in his orange rain jacket standing, apparently, upon the water and waving his oar.

The other boats are turning too, but we are the first to reach the canoe. It is already half full of water and the waves are breaking over the side, threatening to swamp it. The engine has failed and Scotty is pumping furiously.

"It's coming in faster than I can get it out," he tells Skip.

Oddly, he is still smiling. He is 21, and, in spite of his blonde beard, looks younger–an attractive, pink-cheeked youth, forever cheerful. He reminds me of Peggy Anne, who seems to have a permanent smile painted across her face. Peggy Anne cannot help smiling, even when she is mad at somebody or, more surprisingly, when she believes that a ghost or a witch or a vampire is lurking in the woods, ready to jump out at her. It is not an impish grin, like Perri's or Patsie's, but a true smile, like her mother's–sunny, open and innocent, full of trust and good humour. It is more than a smile; it is an attitude. Scotty has it, too, and now in the midst of adversity he does not lose it.

"Can you make it over to land?" Skip asks. "There's some shelter behind that point. We can tow you."

"I think so," says Scotty, still pumping.

The Slush Box takes him in tow and we go ahead in Miss Bardahl. The shore is covered in driftwood and by the time Scotty is pulled in, we have an enormous fire going.

Paul and I are remarkably dry, partly because we have more effective rain gear and partly because we are in the fastest boat. The occupants of The Pig are soaked to the skin. The waters of the lake are close to freezing. Perri and Peggy Anne are crying with the cold and the others are miserable, numbed by the constant battering of the waves in their faces, plastering their hair and running down their necks. Even their shoes are full of water and as they stand huddled round the fire it seems impossible for them to warm up. They have been literally sitting in the lake because the slower Pig does not flush out as easily as the faster boats. Paul, however, is in great spirits.

"Rationale, Mum!" he shouts. "Open up the rationale!"

It is a word he has invented to describe the emergency rations that Janet doles out daily to each boat: mainly raisins and chocolate bars. To Paul and his younger sisters, their ritual consumption has become the highlight of the trip. They live from hour to hour, expectantly awaiting the next piece of mushy chocolate, and years from now, when somebody mentions this river journey, they will probably think of Rowntree's York Dark or Neilson's Burnt Almond.

Patsie, who eats no meat or fish, cannot fathom her younger brother's obsession. But I sympathize with Paul for at his age it was my obsession, too. When I recall my boyhood in the Yukon and my early teens in Victoria, I conjure it up in terms of confections (just as I conjure up my later teens in terms of popular songs). When I think of a certain walk with my mother up the Moosehide Trail behind Dawson, I think of toffee rolls; it is the earliest memory I have—

a memory of a memory, really, for I was only two years old at the time; but I can still remember unwrapping each piece of toffee as we sat on two rocks by the side of the trail and how they tasted. When I think of those hot summer days in Dawson, when we hid under the shade of the wooden sidewalks, I think of the ice cream cones which the B & F Store sold, two for a quarter, and which were made of condensed milk. (It was a long time before I grew used to the comparatively mild taste of "Outside ice cream.") When I think of taking the ferry across the river and hiking through the hills to the old shipyard, where the carcasses of the *Julia B.* and the *Schwatka* sat on the ways, I think of two square chocolate bars called Pieface and Fat Emma. Newly introduced, one was made of dark chocolate wrapped around marshmallow and nuts, the other of milk chocolate, filled with caramel. Whenever I think of those old and battered steamboats, on which we used to play *(I'm captain! I'm captain! . . . No— you was captain last time; I'm captain!)*, the sweet, gooey taste of those chocolate bars comes back to me.

To this day I connect the station at Banff with Coca Cola. There was no Coca Cola in the Yukon and, though I had seen advertisements for it on the backs of magazines, I was never quite sure what it was. Svelte women in cloche hats were depicted drinking it, accompanied by young men with high starched collars and profiles of incredible regularity. It could not, then, be ordinary soda pop because that was something children drank on August 17, Discovery Day, the big fall festival that marked the original discovery of gold on Bonanza creek. This was a day of footraces and dancing and a good deal of drinking by the adult population and the consumption of staggering quantities of free pop by the children. The pop was dispensed from a booth in Minto Park by a Mr. Schwartz, who made some of it himself, and the wonderful thing was that you could have all you wanted. The kind that Mr. Schwartz made was strawberry, very sweet and fizzy, but there was also Orange Kist and Cream Soda and a brown variety with a complicated name that escapes me, the label of which extolled its therapeutic qualities and showed a drawing of a man with a handlebar mustache, wearing an undershirt and flexing his muscles. This we kept until the following day and drank very slowly over a period of several hours, shaking it from time to time to make it fizz, and examining ourselves to see if its health-giving properties were taking effect. But of Coca Cola there was not a drop in Dawson. It was not until I had turned 11, and our family made a trip to the Outside world, and I was exposed to a series of wonders I did not know existed, that I drank a Coca Cola for the first time. I remember being told by an experienced boy, who had been Outside any number of times, that you could buy a bottle of pop for a nickel, but I did not believe him. There were no nickels in Dawson and no dimes, either. The smallest coin was a two-bit piece; that was what you paid for pop, except on Discovery Day. But in Banff, when the train stopped at the station and my father was re-examining the miracle of the Rockies, I slipped inside the lunchroom with my nickel and, sure enough, was able to purchase a bottle of Coca Cola. The taste was extraordinary, being nothing like Mr. Schwartz's strawberry pop or anything else I had ever sampled. I have drunk a fair amount of Coca Cola since that day but have never been able to conjure up the original flavour; perhaps they have changed the formula. At any rate, I understand Paul for my own childhood was a succession of Oh Henry! bars, Lucky Pops, Sweet Maries, humbugs, lemon sticks, jaw-breakers, peppermint-flavoured wax teeth, chocolate-covered cherries, Rowntree's Plain York bar with Your Extra Piece and then Another Extra Piece,

Lowney's Creamy Toffee (covered with bits of hair and cloth from your pocket), licorice whips and whistles that froze brittle in the winter and had to be thawed out in the mouth, ju-jubes, sherbet powders sucked through a straw, comfits with mottoes on them, hard mints, and, of course, Canada Dry gingerale, which was served only on Christmas Day and always made my nose ache in the most wonderful manner.

Paul gets his way and Janet passes out chocolate bars and dried fruit, the only lunch we can manage today. I choose an Oh Henry! because the taste of it takes me back to a certain picnic with my family to the Midnight Dome, the highest point above the town, when we were each allowed a slice of an Oh Henry! bar. I munch on mine and see once again, in memory's eye, the Klondike river below us, choked with tailing piles, and hear, in memory's ear, the whine of a distant gold dredge – that banshee sound of screaming cables borne on the wind, which used to terrify me as a child, because I thought of the dredge as a living monster – and far below, in the streets of Dawson, the rattle of a livery wagon and the sound of voices. In the North the air is so clear that a man standing on this hill above the town can sometimes overhear a conversation in the street far below.

"It looks to me like she's a little calmer," Skip is saying. "It's hard to tell from here but it doesn't look too bad out there. What do you think?"

I think we should press on, before the wind springs up again. Though the lake is still choppy, the fury has abated and Scotty has fixed his motor. We douse the fire and tumble into the boats, but not before an extra ration of chocolate is divided among us.

The surface is bumpy but navigable, and within an hour we have reached the end of the lake and the ghost settlement of Lower Laberge. Here on a deserted bank some of the children spy a little white table, sitting all by itself as if waiting for guests who will never arrive. It is such a curious sight that they insist on bringing the boat closer for a better look and Penny, the film buff, constructs in her imagination a Fellini-like sequence in which, as we move closer, the table is seen to be laid with white linen and silver candlesticks and an untouched pheasant under glass. Furniture in the wilderness is not new to me, though. It forms part of the backdrop of my boyhood: tables and chairs, bedsteads and stools, armoires and sideboards rising out of the tall grasses; locomotive engines rusting in the woods; boarded-up stores chockful of the discarded paraphernalia of the goldrush: couches, gold pans, seltzer bottles, hand organs, grand pianos, Yukon stoves, chimney lamps, walking sticks, flowered chamber pots and glassware; cabins, their doors swinging permanently open to reveal a jumble of old newspapers, discarded letters, fading calendars, unstuffed mattresses and peeling wallpaper. In Dawson we lived surrounded by old machinery that no longer worked. Rusting boilers, huge cogwheels, gears, axles, frayed belting, pumps and pieces of dredges, drive-shafts, pistons and engines of every description were piled in hedgerows along the streets and the riverbank. Behind the school were great boilers, half hidden by the willow, so big a boy could (and did) hide inside them and beside these boilers were massive keystone drills, around which we clambered, playing at cops and robbers. Across the Klondike river lay the remains of a railway: passenger cars, green with age, lined up in the bushes and a pump car that actually worked sat on a small stretch of track beside Bonanza creek. A little white table all alone on a beach is no surprise to anyone brought up in a decaying mining town.

Now, on our right we see another odd spectacle. Like a vast, wooden whale, the hull of an old *Casca* looms out of the willows. There were three steamboats successively named *Casca* but all are fused in my memory as a single stern-wheeler. It is hard to connect this rotting hull with the proud ship, pennants flying, whistle sounding, paddlewheel whirling, that was generally the first to round the Dawson bluffs in the spring after the ice had broken in the river.

In those days, when winter sealed us off from the world, the arrival of the *Casca* signalled the arrival of summer and caused a wave of excitement to sweep over the town. We had not seen fresh fruit since the previous fall. Now great piles of it would grace Apple Jimmy Oglow's stand across from the steamboat docks on Front Street. Familiar faces, driven from the town by the onset of winter, would reappear. American tourists from California and Texas would mingle with us briefly, snap their pictures in front of Robert Service's log cabin and spend their money in the souvenir shops. On boat nights there would be dances for the tourists in the Arctic Brotherhood Hall and in the movie house we called the D-Three-A's—the letters standing for the defunct Dawson Amateur Athletic Association. The *Casca* represented our link with the Outside. As long as the river was open and the steamboat whistle could be heard, we knew we were tied to civilization. When the ice floes began to drift past town and the last boat chugged out onto the grey river under the grey clouds of October, then we realized we were again in prison.

The sound of that first whistle in early June was as musical as the robin's first call. Those three long blasts would electrify the town. One Sunday morning my sister and I set off for Sunday School and had barely reached the church door when the *Casca*'s whistle sounded. St. Paul's Anglican church sits almost on the very rim of the river bank and as we looked south we could see the familiar white wood-smoke moving along behind the islands; and then the big yellow stack itself came into view. The church service, which preceded Sunday School, was still in progress but within moments the congregation broke from the double doors and raced down Front Street towards the White Pass dock. My sister and I and our friend, Axel Nordling, were borne along on the wave. We stood in the crowd on the wharf, marvelling as the big boat puffed in. A rope was thrown out and snubbed tightly, the gangplank rattled down and the passengers moved off. The freight doors opened and we could see crates of fruit – bananas, apples, oranges, even grapes – being trundled over to Apple Jimmy's. There would be no Sunday School that day; our collection money – fifty cents and twenty-five cents respectively – burned in our pockets.

The Sunday School lessons that winter had featured Eve's fall from grace and Christ's temptation in the wilderness and so we were well versed in the ways of Satan. He could appear in any guise in any place and on this warm June morning, in front of the fruit store, Satan took the earthly mask of Axel Nordling. He even *looked* like the devil, with his sharp features and his Scandinavian nose.

"You got collection money?" Axel asked and we nodded, nervously.

"Won't be any collection today," Axel reminded us.

"Let's go inside, look around," Axel suggested. In we went, with the scent of fresh lemons and oranges in our nostrils and the sight of polished apples, Mackintoshes, Delicious, Spies and Gravensteins, dazzling our eyes. But more than anything there were the bananas, hanging in fat clusters from the ceiling.

"Buy a banana," Axel whispered.

"Can't."

"You got money."

"It's for collection."

"There's no collection. Say you gave it anyway. Buy a banana. Just one."

We bought just one; but one wasn't enough. Then we bought another. Then we bought two apples and some grapes and, in an orgy of buying, spent the whole seventy-five cents. We were afraid to go home for lunch. Lunch was fruit, fresh from the *Casca,* fresh from the Outside world, which I could scarcely remember and my sister could not really remember at all. When we did go home for supper we were put to bed and left to contemplate our sins. Our weak excuses were not believed; no doubt we smelled of bananas and oranges. In the years that followed we continued to play with Axel Nordling, but sometimes when I looked at him I thought I could see horns protruding from his forehead and a forked tail at his rear.

The hulk of the *Casca* retreats into the distance as we enter that stretch of the Yukon river system known as the Thirtymile, that being the distance from the end of the lake to the Yukon's first great tributary, the Teslin. To me, this is the most beautiful section of the river. Here the channel is narrow and winding, coiling under high banks and through flatland. The scenery changes constantly, each bend in the river bringing a surprise. The water is blue and so clear that you can often see the bottom, and in dark corners, the Arctic grayling lies waiting for the hook. The Thirtymile is also considered to be the most dangerous section of the river because of the hairpin turns. During the stampede many boats, from scows to sternwheelers, foundered here.

In 1898 my father's party almost lost one of their boats in the Thirtymile. It struck a rock and stove a hole in its bottom, causing a two-day delay. In that hectic summer, the river was alive with all manner of craft. I remember him telling me of a strange sight which he did not report in his diary. At one point, he said, he had looked into the clear waters of the Thirtymile and seen a scow with thirty dead bodies lying on the bottom. My eyes went as round as Peggy Anne's when she listens to a ghost story and then, with a slow smile, my father explained that these were the bodies of beef cattle, drowned on their way to Dawson.

We are not going to explore the Thirtymile today because the company is still wet and cold from the lake. A few miles down the river is the best campsite we have yet found and though we have to lug our kit and stores up a high bank, the view is worth the effort. We gaze down upon the ribbon of the Yukon, glittering in the evening sunlight and winding off between the wooded hills. Beneath our feet is a dense carpet of moss – a natural mattress on which to pitch the tents. Janet, who thinks of everything, has brought along several lengths of nylon clothesline for an emergency. It is needed: everything in Patsie's pack, for instance, is sopping. She and the others huddle round the fire to dry and later on, with characteristic good cheer, Patsie draws that scene for the log.

All the new boxes Janet has scrounged in Whitehorse have been reduced to mush and so we must make do with garbage bags for the rest of the trip. Fortunately she has brought dozens of them. She, Pamela and Penny find the package marked DAY FOUR and we have smoked country sausage, sizzling in the pan, with fresh cornbread made by Pamela, who has been planning that surprise all day. Pamela (whom Peter calls "Dorothy Domestic") has determined upon a series of culinary coups – home baked beans, split pea soup, spaghetti Bolognese, curried chicken, cake and even bread. I think again of my parents taking the loaves to bed with them so that they could rise under the blankets, and the repeated references in my father's 1898 diary to biscuits baked along the way.

Patsie has found a separate place on the fire for her vegetable stew. All the cooking utensils are in use, tainted with meat juices, but she has foraged in the woods and found a small aluminum pot, complete with handle, lying among the mosses. It is an eerie discovery. Here on the bank we can look out on the empty river and on the endless hills drifting off to the north, ridge upon ridge, all the way to the Arctic. There is no hint of man – no boat upon the swift waters, golden now in the rays of the late evening sun, no smudge of smoke staining the far horizon where the spiky spruces meet the pale sky, not even a clearing in the forest or an old blaze on a tree. But there is the little aluminum pot, and a serviceable one, too, lying in the moss. At one of our last camping spots the children came upon a wooden rocking horse in the woods. How did it get there? We can only know that others have passed this way and left these tantalizing hints of their presence.

We sit around the fire, reviewing the events of the day when, out of nowhere, the rain hits us. We leave our mugs of coffee and scramble for the clothesline. Just as suddenly the downpour subsides and there, arching across the river, is a rainbow. It sets the mood for the evening. We add a little rum to the coffee and begin to sing – Scout songs from my day and from Peter's and Paul's, and old army songs and school songs and crazy songs.

Peter leads the assembly in a nonsense song, for which everybody has to supply a verse:

> PETER: I know a guy whose name is Skip!
> CHORUS: Hey, Lawdy, Lawdy-oh!
> PETER: Boy, is he an awful drip!

63

CHORUS: Hey, Lawdy, Lawdy-oh!
        Hey, Lawdy, Lawdy, Lawdy!
        Hey, Lawdy, Lawdy-oh!
        Hey, Lawdy, Lawdy, Lawdy!
        Hey, Lawdy, Lawdy-oh!

Enormous glee from the smaller children at this insult!

PATSIE: I know a gal whose name is Penny!
CHORUS: Hey, Lawdy, Lawdy-oh!
PATSIE: When it comes to brains she ain't got any!
CHORUS: Hey, Lawdy, Lawdy-oh!

Pandemonium from the little girls at this scurrilous attack on brainy Penny! And so the doggerel continues, lampooning Ross (hair like moss), Scotty (very naughty), Cheri (they claim she's smart but she's not very) and all the others until little Perri, her black face glowing in the firelight and her curly mop standing out from her head in a dark halo, pipes up:

PERRI: I know a lady name is Jan!
CHORUS: Hey, Lawdy, Lawdy-oh!
PERRI: I keep hearing her say: 'Goddam!'
CHORUS: Hey, Lawdy, Lawdy-oh!

It breaks us up and Perri, who is a bit of a ham, grins at the attention. Suddenly, through the adversity of the rain, and the danger on the lake, we have become a tightly knit company, knowing each other intimately enough to trade insults in song. Nicknames are being coined, slogans developed, legends established. Years from now, if Perri or Peter should happen to encounter Scotty or Ross, it will be necessary only to whisper: "Lawdy, Lawdy-oh!" to bring this night on the river crowding back, the night of the rainbow and Pamela's cornbread and the sing-song round the campfire.

DAY FIVE

Skip has come up with a system for getting away earlier. As soon as he shouts "rise and shine," each of us will immediately pack up our kit and take it down to the boats. Then the empty tents can be struck by one work party while another prepares breakfast.

"Rise and shine!" Skip cries. It is seven and the sun is out. There are groans from the boys' tent but almost immediately the small figure of Perri appears. She is dollar bright and fully dressed, right down to her life belt. Off she goes, dragging her kitbag down the bank, following Skip's plan to the letter. She cannot lift the bag so she half pushes and half pulls it through the moss.

"Perri, what makes that bag of yours so heavy?"

"It's the cheese, Dad."

My God, the cheese! We have forgotten about the extra cheese! Janet packed some perishables, including two great wheels of cheddar, in the children's bags rather than send them weeks ahead to Bennett. One cheese has been retrieved and partly eaten but we have forgotten the other and Perri has been packing it around for four days without complaint.

"I'll take the cheese, Perri."

"Okay, Dad."

Now, for the first time, she is able to lift her own kitbag.

"Everything I wear smells of cheese," she says as she trots off. It is a statement of fact, not a complaint.

The others are slowly rising and shining and thanks to the new system we cut forty minutes off our departure time. This morning we will not use the motors. We will lie lazily in the boats and let the current take us down the Thirtymile.

Every river has a personality of its own, but the Yukon has more than most because its character changes as it grows, broadening and maturing on its long journey to the sea. The Mackenzie is a majestic river but a monotonous one. It flows directly to the Arctic, almost in a straight line, with scarcely a curve and rarely a twist, moving resolutely on beside the long line of the accompanying mountains. It is much the same with the St. Lawrence and the Saskatchewan. But the Yukon is more human. It has many moments of uncertainty and some of frivolity. It skitters back and forth, hesitates, changes its mind, charges forward, then retreats. On the Yukon there is rarely a dull moment: new vistas and fresh terrains open up behind every curve. This is because the river has embarked on a long and wearying quest. The Mackenzie rises in the hinterland and sets out in a direct line for the Arctic, sensing exactly where its goal must be, but the Yukon does not appear to know. It rises within fifteen miles of the Pacific but its search for that same ocean takes it in the opposite direction. Like a prospector seeking hidden gold it explores the land, swinging this way and that, pushing its way through obstacles, circumnavigating others, following false scents and lost trails, growing from infancy to youth to maturity to old age. Here, between Laberge and the Teslin, it is like a child, the water crystal clear, pure to drink and blue as Peggy Anne's eyes. It wriggles about like a child in delight. Later, when the first of the great tributaries pours in, it will begin to broaden and then, with the alluvial muds

66

of the Pelly and the White joining it, will lose the colour of its youth, and become wider, almost fleshy, the great islands and sandbars giving it texture. By the time it reaches Dawson it is in the first flush of its early maturity, a noble river, flowing confidently past the town, giving only passing notice to the little Klondike, which foams out of the hills to greet it. But it has a long way to go yet. On its huge arc through Alaska it must force a narrow passage through the Ramparts and then spread out, miles wide, over the Yukon flats. Here the Arctic beckons and the river noses north across the Circle, only to discover that its instincts are wrong and that it must retreat south and west, growing broader as others join it, until at Norton Sound it divides into numberless, nameless channels to mingle at last with the cold sea.

It is a new sensation to drift with the current. After the cough and sputter of the engines, this soft and leisurely progress down the river is utterly relaxing. There is no sound except our voices and the hissing of the water. We can converse easily and call from boat to boat. In the wider parts of the river we can hear our echo against the high banks. As we drift, the boats describe great circles so that we see the river and the scenery from various angles.

Craggy rocks, plumed with evergreens, rise from the water. Around the next corner, the river passes under clay banks, three hundred feet high. Mixed in with the dark spruces are the bleached trunks of birches and the olive greens of aspen poplars, many of them notched by the teeth of beaver. At times we seem to be plunging directly through the dark forest, the river no more than sixty feet wide and shaded by the trees; at others the channel broadens into flat meadows; then again, the high, eroded banks return, pocked by swallows' nests and marked by mud slides. We will come upon these clay cliffs again and again as we drift north.

Beneath our boats we can hear the water seething and hissing. Peggy Anne says that it looks like water boiling in a kettle. Somewhere below, the grayling are lurking but the boys, who have several rods out, have had no luck yet. Peter is casting expertly from Miss Bardahl and now he feels a tug on his line. Enormous excitement! A moment later he lands a fat, foot-long grayling, detaches it neatly from the hook and waves it aloft for the others to see.

It is not surprising that Peter should catch the first fish for he understands and enjoys mechanical techniques. At home he has a workbench and a set of tools. Like my father, but unlike me, he can do anything with his hands. My father had once been a carpenter's apprentice and I can remember him patiently trying to teach me how to make a mortice-and-tenon joint and how to dovetail drawers with a chisel but I was no good at that. If he was disappointed, he did not show it. He was forever building things. Once, when we camped at Rock Creek in the Klondike valley, he built a scale model of a Roman catapult, for my sister and me, explaining, of course, the history and uses of the weapon. After the D.A.A.A. theatre showed Douglas Fairbanks in *The Three Musketeers,* and every kid in town became a duellist, he made me a beautiful wooden sword with a guard fashioned from a Hills Brothers coffee tin. When we children grew too old to occupy cribs in our parents' bedroom, he added an extra room to our house. I can still see him working away with plane and chisel and finishing off the porch railing with a little fretwork.

The most magnificent and satisfying thing he built was a boat. It was a proper boat – not a scow of the kind constructed on the lakes in 1898, but a handsome twenty-six foot motorboat, with a round bottom and a forward storage cuddy. He rented an abandoned hotel on Front Street and every weekend and most evenings for about a year he laboured in this makeshift workshop on his boat. We children would bring him down his lunch and sit around watching him bend each rib to the required curvature by soaking it in water and forcing it into a pattern between two confining rows of nails. When it was finished, he called it *The Bluenose*, after the famous schooner, and painted the prow a bright blue.

The four or five summers that followed must have been the happiest in my parents' life. We lived on the river. Almost every day, when he finished work, we would pack a picnic and set out for one of the Yukon's many islands. In July we would pitch a permanent tent on one of these islands and camp there, my father commuting to work by boat. Thus I came to know the river in all its moods. As the water dropped in the summer, divided islands would be joined by spits of sand in which warm ponds would be left behind for bathing. Between the larger islands were sloughs, some of them shallow enough to wade across, so that you could sometimes move from island to island, wading and walking. There were fish in some of the smaller tributaries, in Swede creek, for instance, and in the famous Indian river–dark, beautiful streams near whose mouths one could find limpid pools.

Drifting down the Thirtymile it all comes back to me: the familiar Yukon hills, their erosion creases choked with evergreens; the little pup creeks gurgling down through the thick forests; the bank swallows pouring from their cliffside caves and filling the air with chatter; the great bluffs around which the river courses and eddies, so that the water, in some places, is going in two directions at once. This is the river of my childhood and of my dreams, for it has often returned, grotesquely distorted, to haunt my adult sleep.

The temperature has risen to 75, the sun is baking our

skin, and the fishermen are busy. By lunchtime we have four grayling. By the time lunch is over, we have eight, caught near the bank between bites of sandwiches. In the afternoon, there are other excitements. The lead boat spies four cow moose, grazing in the swampy mouth of a small creek. They look up from their foraging, their shovel snouts dripping weeds, inspect us curiously with their great, soft eyes and then lope leisurely away as the river sweeps us past. Then, in the space of a few minutes, we spot no fewer than three bald eagles in the sky. On the eroding left bank stands a lone cabin, tottering on the very lip, about to plunge into the river; a former steamboat refuelling station. After that we sweep around the great u.s. Bend, where the river forms a tight "S" between high, brooding cliffs.

An hour later we come upon an Indian camp and smoke rack. We beach the boats and walk up to greet a family of four. Long strips of moosemeat hang from the outer rack, drying in the sun, while on the inner rack halves of salmon are turning dark red over a wood fire. We buy a smoked salmon for two dollars and continue on our way. Behind us, we can see the blue smoke drifting out of the forest and mingling with the blue of the sky – the only evidence of human life we have seen all day.

In mid-afternoon we reach the end of the Thirtymile and the mouth of the Teslin, or Hootalinqua. Here, in 1898, the boats that were built by the men who crossed the White and Chilkoot passes joined the boats of the men who came up the Spectral Trail from Ashcroft or up the Stikine or Skeena rivers and trekked overland to Teslin lake. Opposite the Teslin's mouth, clinging to the left bank of the Yukon, are the old buildings of Hootalinqua Station, one of more than a dozen ghost settlements that dot the river between Whitehorse and Dawson, all of them tenantless since the highway put the steamboats out of business. We pull up the boats and explore the empty community. The old Mounted Police post is half hidden by the Yukon's official flower, the crimson fireweed. The blooms reach up to the empty windows, almost touching the grasses that hang down from the crumbling roof.

On an island opposite Hootalinqua Post, an odd sight catches our eye. Above the willows and aspens we see a great smoke-stack. We nose into the beach and make our way into the woods. There, rising above us several storeys high, with willows poking through the holes in her deck, is an entire steamboat. She is very old, the paint long gone from her hull, but intact except for the paddlewheel, which lies in pieces beside her. She is called *The Evelyn* and a plaque on her hull proclaims that she is under the protection of the Territorial Government. There is a similar placard on the Hootalinqua police post and on every other ghost town along the river. It is about all the local government can do at the moment to draw attention to the fact that these are historic sites worthy of preservation. Unhappily, there is no money yet for restoration.

I have never heard of *The Evelyn*. She did not ply the river in my day. Later on I learn that she was purchased in 1922 by the White Pass company, which ran the steamboats and the trains, but having bought her they found they had no use for her. She has been here ever since, with the brambles growing round her and the willows growing through her and only her smoke-stack protruding from the new growth on an island that was once a bustling shipyard.

The day is wearing on and Big Salmon, where we expect to camp for the night, is another thirty-five miles downstream, so we turn on the motors and skip along with the current. Five miles farther on we spot more moose, grazing in the backwater at the foot of a steep slide of black clay.

71

But I am not looking at the moose. My chart tells me that the hull of the original *Klondike*, which sank in the Thirty-mile but drifted to this point, lies just under the water at the base of the slide. As the others watch the moose, I spot her, like the shadow of a mammoth fish, outlined by a series of ripples. And now my mind goes back to a summer's day in 1928 when the *Klondike*, fresh from the shipwrights, first puffed into Dawson. She was a freighter, with a big open deck and only a few cabins for passengers – the biggest steamboat on the river then, though not as big as those great Mississippi packets, the *Susie, Sarah* and *Hannah*, that plied these waters in the stampede days. Now, like the *Susie*, which rotted slowly away in the shipyard downriver from Dawson, the *Klondike* is only a hull-shaped ripple in the whispering river.

I think one of the reasons why the steamboats held such a fascination for me was that they represented, in a kind of second-hand way, the mysterious wonders of the Outside, which I only vaguely remembered from my visit at the age of five. Sometimes there would be as many as three stern-wheelers tied to the dock at one time: the *Yukon* from down-river, the *Casca* or the *Whitehorse* from upriver and a freighter, such as the *Klondike*. These boats, which brought fresh fruits, also brought people from far away places. Most of them were American tourists and we thought of them as a different race. "These aliens seem quite friendly," my father heard one of them remark and the phrase tickled him so much that he repeated it many times over the years. We were always polite to the tourists. When they passed me on the streets I spoke to each one and was surprised when they did not always return my greeting. I had been told that on the Outside people did not say hello to every Tom, Dick or Harry they met on the street but I refused to believe that.

My experience was limited to that single journey at the age of five, when we had gone straight to my grandparents' home in Oakville, then a small town. I had no experience of the big city – I had only read about big cities in books – but with all my heart I longed to experience one.

Now, as the Yukon shoreline rolls by me and the river widens and the wooded islands grow more numerous, I think how strange it is that my own children, brought up on the edge of a big city, loathe and despise the metropolis. They seek to escape the asphalt and the highrise, the buzzing traffic and the flashing lights and so this wilderness experience is for them a kind of Elysium, as it is, indeed, for me. Yet when I was their age, enjoying the river almost daily, all the Elysian fields were asphalt. I longed for lights and advertising signs. I longed to ride a streetcar or a railway train. I longed for tall buildings and throngs of people. Most of all I longed for circuses, carnivals, amusement parks, radio and talking pictures, none of which I had ever experienced. Like Coca Cola, they were no more than images in magazines, totally unattainable.

In the fall of 1931, when my father had accumulated enough holiday time and my mother had finished the novel she was writing on the kitchen table (my father typing it out for her each night on the old Remington), the voyage to the Outside at last took shape. We would go to Toronto, live in my Aunt Florrie's house on Huntley Street, visit my mother's parents in Oakville and she would place her novel with a publisher and we would all be rich and would go to circuses and carnivals all day. It did not quite work out that way and yet in retrospect that winter seems to me to have been one long carnival. I saw sights I had never seen before and spectacles that I did not know existed and I developed, belatedly but permanently, a childish delight in things that whirr and buzz and flash and rotate and jiggle. For that is how I saw the Outside: a whirring, buzzing carnival of light.

In the tomb of the Yukon winter, when the smoke rose in perpendicular columns from the chimneys and a chill fog hung like a shroud over the valley, Dawson was as dark and silent as the forests that bore down upon it. Noon was twilight for the six sunless weeks of December and January. The only automobile that dared to venture forth was the one owned by Archie Fournier, who brought around the milk – when there was milk – in beer bottles stopped with old corks, and who cranked his Model T at every house as the steam poured from the radiator. Even the police kept their horses in the stables when the temperature dropped to 40 below so that virtually nothing moved in Dawson and certainly nothing buzzed or flashed except in the week before Christmas when a few mechanical toys went on display in the window of Mme. Tremblay's store.

Outside, everything was different, right down to the milk bottles. I saw my first neon sign in Juneau. It was as exciting to my father as it was to me, for he, too, had never seen one. Of course he knew exactly how it worked and explained it in detail, comparing it to the Northern Lights. We stood under it and watched it wink redly in the night. EATS, is what it said, as it flashed on and off. EATS . . . EATS . . . EATS. Marvelous!

In Toronto there were bigger and better signs – enormous ones advertising various chocolates hanging over Bloor Street. Willards had a gigantic sun made up of hundreds of coloured lights that sent its rays shooting out in every direction; Neilson's had another, showing three shooting stars made up of crimson neon, that darted above our heads. Everything was new to me: milkshakes I had never known made on machines that rotated and buzzed, fizzy drinks called "phosphates," fireworks, cent candy, searchlights, tandem streetcars, roller skates, songs I had never heard before, comics I had never read, talkies I had never seen.

Dawson, in those days, seemed light years behind the world. People still danced the two-step and the one-step in the Arctic Brotherhood Hall. Fashions and popular songs were years old. Until 1926, my mother wore her hair in a bun at the top, like Mrs. Katzenjammer in the funnies, and sang such songs as "After the Ball is Over" and "Ta-ra-ra Boom-de-ay." Movies reached Dawson only after every other theatre on the continent was done with them. We saw Griffith's *Birth of a Nation* in 1929. And there were no talkies.

We were allowed to see movies only rarely and then it was a rule that we must be accompanied by our parents. Once, when the Wolf Cubs were taken on a surprise treat to see a cowboy film, I had to phone home for permission to go. It was given to me, but after the cartoons were finished I noticed my father slip into a seat a few rows behind us. I found it embarrassing at the time but years later I came to understand the reason for it. Dawson's public and commercial buildings were forever burning down and he was deathly afraid of fire in the movie house, and rightly so, for a few years later the D.A.A.A. theatre was destroyed by flames. So there he sat, watching Rex Bell knock down no fewer than seven desperadoes.

"Were there cartoons?" he asked me, after it was over.

"You missed them. There were two: Oswald the Rabbit in *Panicky Pancakes* and *Mississippi Mud*."

"Oh, damn; did I? I'd much rather have seen them than the cowboys."

For anything that was animated fascinated him. He explained to me how cartoons were made and demonstrated the technique by flipping the pages of a book on which he had drawn a bouncing ball. In Toronto, we saw a lot of cartoons and talking pictures and plays and concerts as well.

"The boy is here for an education," he told the principal of Rosedale Public School, "and so I intend to take him out of school whenever necessary. He has a bit of catching up to do."

The principal looked startled but nodded agreement. There was not a great deal he could do since my father had obviously made up his mind. My father was there for an education, too. He signed up for three courses in mathematics and physics at the University of Toronto and went to lectures every day for the sheer enjoyment of it, not in the least bothered by the fact that he was three times the age of his fellow students. "Those fellows are smart as whips," he'd say. "It takes some doing to keep up with them."

He took me out of school whenever something came up that he thought I ought to see. We went to the Passion Play in the Royal Alex and *As You Like It* at Hart House and a wonderful marionette show at Eaton's and the Ice Carnival in the new Maple Leaf Gardens; and we listened to the Hart House String Quartet and saw some new paintings by people called The Group of Seven. We visited Ottawa for the opening of Parliament where George Black, the Member for the Yukon and new Speaker of the House, actually winked at my father as the procession went by. There, in his brother's home, I first tasted French fried potatoes and, more important than Parliament, saw a film called *Union Station*, with Douglas Fairbanks, Jr. and Joan Crawford, both of whom actually talked. My father often picked the movies we would see by finding out what the accompanying cartoons were. We saw the first Silly Symphony ever made, *Skeleton Dance*, at the Uptown, and the second, *The Old Clockmaker*, at the Hollywood, where the feature was *The Smiling*

Lieutenant, starring Maurice Chevalier and Claudette Colbert. And if I remember all these details after forty years, while forgetting other, more important world events and my own schoolwork, it is because they made an enormous impression on a small boy, who had been cooped up for all of his eleven years in a northern mining town.

My mother did not find a publisher for her novel. Oddly, she had not chosen to write about the Yukon, which everyone thought exotic but which she thought commonplace, but about Ontario farm life, which everyone thought commonplace but she thought exotic. She was twenty years away from the North before it occurred to her to tell her own story, which was much more romantic and exciting than anything she tried to make up. We did, however, get to a carnival. When the Sunnyside Amusement Park opened up in the spring my father took my sister and me to the lakeshore and there, for several hours, we rode on every device until we had exhausted the list and ourselves and were sticky from cotton candy and dizzy from being whirled about in things that jiggled and buzzed and bumped and lit up. The memory of that magic afternoon with the lights flashing and the music playing and the air heady with incense of frying onions has never left me and ever since I have had a passion for such places – for amusement parks and world's fairs and Disneylands and exhibitions and sideshows. Like my father, who was 61 at the time and loved every moment of that day (he explained the principle of centrifugal force as we whirled about on the flying swings), I have never been able to get enough of the buzzing and the flashing and the jiggling, perhaps because I had to wait so many years to enjoy it.

Here on the Yukon all these by-products of civilization

seem far away, in time and in geography. We have seen no human sign since we left the Indian family on the Thirty-mile. On we go, round the great bends of the river, each marked on the steamboat charts: Vanmeter Bend and Keno Bend, Glacier Gulch Bend and Big Eddy. On we go past Fife creek and the famous Cassiar Bar, where in the days before the goldrush, the early prospectors made wages panning flour gold, whose lightness brought it down the creeks into the river proper.

In his diary on July 14, 1898 my father recorded that his party had stopped at Cassiar Bar to look at the operations there and "saw plenty of large but light colours in the pan" before they moved on for dinner at the police post at the mouth of the Big Salmon river. We, too, will have dinner at Big Salmon. We reach the river's mouth and there, on the far side, we spy the cabins of the deserted village. And still we have seen no people.

Nothing moves on the river these days. Nothing moves on the banks except the moose, bear and lynx. The cabins grow up out of the grass and the grasses grow up over the cabins, for the roofs are constructed of fertile sod. Within, we find evidence of the past at Big Salmon – old mattresses, brass bedsteads, home-made tables and chairs, and in the trading post, what is left of counter and cupboards. Great salmon racks stand outside near the bank and on these we hang out our clothes to dry.

We have spent some seven hours on the river, an average run, and we are becoming more organized. One crew is at work putting up the tents. Another is cleaning and gutting the grayling for breakfast. A third is bringing up the food and utensils and making a fire. Pamela is preparing a pot of split pea soup using the hambone from a previous meal. And we have the smoked salmon as an unexpected hors d'oeuvre.

Patsie has been given the permanent job of locating and establishing a latrine at each campsite, a task to which she brings both enthusiasm and artistry. Now she comes running down the old path—a path worn smooth for more than fifty years by Indian feet—to announce that she has built the best latrine yet, not too far away and yet secluded, downwind, and, for the first time, with a real log to sit on. She is so proud of her handiwork that a bunch of us accompany her into the woods to inspect the wonderful latrine and offer her congratulations.

We do not linger after dinner. It has been a long and satisfying day and everybody is ready for bed. Only Patsie is still up, drying her damp nightie over the fire. Some of us are already asleep when suddenly we hear her excited shout:

"The Northern Lights, you guys! The Northern Lights!"

We tumble out of the tents and there they are, "literally dancing and playing music," as Patsie describes them in the log—long streaks and curtains of violet and emerald, swirling and shifting across the heavens and making the night almost as bright as the day—giant abstract neon signs, as my father once explained to me, jiggling and flashing and whirling about like a giant carnival in the velvet of the sky.

DAY SIX

Today we cut another half hour from our departure time in spite of the fact that we have fresh grayling for breakfast. It is perhaps the most delicious fish I know but then I have eaten only grayling freshly caught from swift-flowing, ice cold waters. When I was a boy of eight I once consumed eight grayling at a single sitting at a fishing camp on Rock creek, a Klondike tributary. That was the year my sister Lucy caught the largest grayling taken that season from Yukon waters and got her photograph in the Toronto *Globe*. I remember it very well: the small child with the chubby knees holding up the big fish, her large brown eyes, which were her mother's and are now her son's, squinting slightly beneath her bangs as she looked into the sun. My Aunt Maude was not amused: "Teaching the child to torture animals!" she said with a snort—or so I heard later.

I am not a fisherman. I have caught only one grayling in my life and that was under very odd circumstances during the Goldrush Festival in Dawson in 1962. The town was full of newspaper cronies, all of whom had brought along fishing tackle. They treated me as an expert and asked where the best spots were. I had no idea what to tell them until I remembered that fishing camp on Rock creek and so I promised that I would lead them to a place where they could catch grayling. I found Rock creek easily enough, but there was no evidence of any fishing camp; one twist of the stream looked very much like another. Where was the bank from which my little sister had caught that enormous fish? Where was the site of George Jeckell's lodge, which my family used to visit on certain summer weekends and where my father had once constructed for us that marvellous Roman catapult? Of these there was no sign. Unmarked by man's presence, the creek raced over its gravel bed between clumps of willows and it was as if no fisherman had ever waded in its waters. I decided I must make good on my pledge and, selecting a likely-looking curve, announced that this was the spot for grayling. The assembly gave me the honour of the first cast. I managed somehow to fling my line out into the water without snagging it on a willow and, to my absolute astonishment, felt an answering tug. A moment later I had a grayling wriggling on the moss. The effect was perhaps the most dramatic and satisfying that I have ever known. I could feel waves of admiration radiating from my audience. I declined to fish further, having made my point, but the others cast all afternoon without being rewarded by so much as a bite. Then as we prepared to leave, an old timer came loping by and gazed on us as if we were demented. "What're you doing fishing here?" he asked. "Hasn't been a grayling caught in this area for more than twenty-five years." Well, yes, there had been, we told him. Just one.

The boats are packed and everyone is clamouring to sit with everyone else in any boat except The Pig. I split the party into evenly weighted groups: "Mom can ride up with Pamela and Patsie this time. I'll take The Slush Box with Penny and the two Deaners. The Wows can all go in The Pig."

As the expected chorus of protest arises from the Wows, I realize I have unconsciously adopted the special argot of our voyage. For reasons that have little logic behind them, the two little girls are known as the Deaners while the four boys: Robert, Peter, Berton and Paul, are called "Wows." Both names come from Peter, a born mimic, who has for days been imitating people he knows whom he designates as Wows. The other boys have turned the word into adjective and verb as well as noun. Now they are all known as Wows and will be for the rest of the voyage and, when they meet up from time to time, perhaps for the rest of their lives. After all, most proud and closely knit institutions adopt a secret language and families are no exception.

And so we drift off down the widening Yukon, the Deaners in one boat, the Wows in another. It is a glorious day. Beside me, Penny has taken out a bottle of shampoo and now she leans over the edge, dips her head in the cold water and begins to wash her long hair. Up front, in the canoe, Scotty has hung out his washing to dry. Beside me, the little Deaners are singing to each other. Paul, in The Pig, begins his regular chant about "rationale!" The nearest settlement, indeed the only one in five hundred miles, is seventy-seven miles downstream and it is more than possible that you could go seventy-seven miles in every direction and hear no other human voices.

"It's just so peaceful and beautiful up here," Patsie writes in the log. "There are sandy cliffs eroding down into the river, huge, weird-shaped mountains, and aspen overtaking black spruce."

Is it here, or farther upstream, I wonder, that the big dam is talked about—the giant project that would turn all of the upper river into one gigantic reservoir? Laberge would vanish into the mother lake and so would the Thirtymile.

82

Below the dam, this great river would be reduced to a trickle. Mud flats, dried-up channels, hedgerows of drowned trees— all these by-products of civilization and progress, which I have seen to my horror in British Columbia, would be the legacy of the power interests. Worse, history itself would be obliterated as it has already been obliterated by the great dredges that tore up the valleys of the Klondike watershed.

And this is a curious thing. After a certain interval, junk becomes treasure. In the Middle East that transformation took several thousand years; in the Yukon, not much more than half a century. Skip Burns is already searching the forests for pink insulators, which can be seen occasionally clinging to the tops of the trees, marking the route of the old telegraph line between Whitehorse and Dawson. In less than a decade, these have become prizes. In my boyhood, we were surrounded by junk, much of which would be priceless today. Across from Billy Biggs' blacksmith shop on Third Avenue stood the old Red Feather Saloon, boarded up and jammed to the ceiling with all manner of strange odds and ends. Hidden beneath the heaps of gold pans and picks was an ancient piano, which nobody bothered with until my friend Bob Darch, the ragtime entertainer, came through town in the Fifties, rummaged beneath the rubble and discovered it was a rare five-pedal Cornish, one of only three ever built. He bought it cheaply, cleaned it up, made it part of his night club act and turned down an offer of three thousand dollars for it. When my father was building his boat in the abandoned hotel on Front Street, my sister and I, rummaging through the accumulated waste at the rear, came upon a thick package of old letters tied with a pink ribbon. They turned out to be love letters, written in 1898 by a prospector on the creeks and sent to a dancehall soubrette in Dawson. We read a few of them—two small children giggling among the cobwebs and sawdust–then threw them away. What would I not give to have them now! In 1954, on Sourdough Gulch, a pup of Bonanza, Colin Low of the National Film Board while making a documentary about the stampede found in a disused cabin a book titled *The Politics of Labour* by Phillips Thompson. Phillips Thompson was my maternal grandfather and the book was autographed and inscribed to my father on the occasion of his marriage to my mother. He had been working on the steam points that summer, thawing ground for the dredge, and, since he had no money, he and my mother had spent their honeymoon in a tent on Sourdough Gulch. No doubt he had lent the book to a neighbour and did not get it back. When Colin found it, the book had been lying on the cabin floor, untouched, for forty-four years. But then, in my boyhood, every cabin contained such curiosities, and there were thousands of cabins and thousands of picks and thousands of wheelbarrows and thousands of shovels, all scattered about on the floors of the famous creeks–bric-a-brac of every kind, some of it worthless and some of it no doubt priceless, littering the countryside. The individual miners had taken all the gold they could find and departed and, because high freight rates made it impossible to take very much with them, they had left almost everything behind–tinned food, beds and mattresses, books and magazines, letters and documents, pictures and photographs, mining equipment of every description and even musical instruments. To be sure, they had ripped open the ground, slashed down the trees, sullied the clear streams and scarred the landscape. But this pollution was as nothing compared to the ravages that followed when the great dredges were built. Then came the brush-cutting crews, stripping the land of every scrap of green growth and, following them, the bulldozers, knocking down the cabins and after the bulldozers the hydraulic monitors whose jets of water could cut a man in two; and after the nozzles had torn off the rich topsoil and sent it rushing down the creeks towards the river, the thawing crews arrived to turn each valley into a sea of mud – a hideous scar from rimrock to rimrock, but so pliable that the dredge could bite into it and retrieve what gold was left by the miners. Thus almost all evidence of the historic stampede was obliterated from Bonanza and Eldorado, Last Chance and Gold Bottom, Gold Run, Hunker, Dominion, Sulphur and Quartz creeks. Only in the high benchland and in the dead little towns along the old roads can you find the occasional cabin that dates back before the century. Was all this ruin worth the gold that was left? Or would the relics of the stampede have been more valuable in the long run? The curious thing is that the dredges themselves, having been rendered obsolete when the gold finally ran out a decade ago, have themselves become archaeology. The biggest of them all, which lies half sunken in the baked mud of Bonanza like some trapped dinosaur, has become a prime tourist attraction. Visitors pour out to gaze up at it, towering several storeys above their heads. Children clamber up the links of its giant securing chains – each link as tall as a school-age boy. Its stacker, which once spewed out a steady shower of gravel dross, hangs over the road like a brooding presence. And its buckets, which once bit deep into the bedrock and ripped up the land, have been dismantled and used as road markers. The dredge has become history and if admission were charged to view it, might eventually bring in as much gold from the pockets of the curious as it once dug out of the old creeks.

While I am pondering these paradoxes we have come into the lee of Dutch Bluff, an immense escarpment around which the river sweeps in a wide arc known as Fourth of July Bend, and there, at the far end of the arc, half submerged in the sand on our right, is the rusting outline of an old dredge. I did not know that there were any dredges working the Yukon river itself and I do not know the history of this one but I see that it is marked on the steamboat charts, which means that it has been here for a very long time, a prehistoric monster, all skeleton and no flesh. It was probably here in the days when our family drifted down the river and almost certainly was here when my father came down alone in the *Bluenose.* Dredges were commonplace pieces of machinery in those days.

One of my regrets is that I did not go with him on that last voyage. My mother was not enthusiastic about the idea; she loved the river but also lived in terror that it would claim one of her children as it had claimed more than one of her friends. Our doctor had vanished into the river one summer during a canoe trip and only his dog was found. Later, the river took Harry Francis, the teamster who had been one of my father's party on that original voyage in 1898. It is cold enough to paralyze you in a few moments and angry enough to suck you under forever should you tumble from your boat. My mother was afraid of that. On the family trip in 1926 I had been frighteningly restless, continually jumping up and leaning over and putting my hands in the water against all orders until I was confined to a small space in the bow, behind a seat, from where I could not squirm out. I was older when my father made his proposal, but still she feared that without another person in the boat, my father, busy in the stern, would not be able to control me. He did not argue but he was determined to make the trip anyway and so it was decided that he would go on ahead of us, for he had a work deadline to meet. He would take his boat down the river and we would follow some time later by steamboat, after a stopover in Vancouver.

He had the *Bluenose* shipped to Whitehorse and from there made his way down the Yukon all alone, loving every minute of it. For the river in those days was very much alive. At Big Salmon and Hootalinqua and Yukon Crossing, at Fort Selkirk and Minto and Stewart City, there would be people on the bank to greet him. They would know him well and he would know them all, too. After thirty years he knew everyone in the Territory; many of them had filed mining claims in his recorder's office in Dawson. The journey down the river would be for him a journey of renewal, allowing him to live again the days of the stampede and the days of the family trip and to greet acquaintances and old friends whom he had not seen in decades. In between the larger communities were single cabins and here it was obligatory to stop; a man living for months in the wilderness was starved for company and for news and it was an act of cruelty to ignore him. I can remember seeing them tearing down from their cabins at the sight of our boat and waving wildly and shouting their heads off, fearful that we might pass them by; and then, when we landed, pressing food and drink upon us and urging us to stay the night and pleading, almost with tears in their eyes, for us to tarry a little longer, and running after us down the bank as we left, crying "Please don't go yet! Not yet!" So for my father a journey down the river would be like a stroll down a familiar street and I wish I could have gone with him, although I do not blame my mother since she acted out of love.

While my father navigated the river we stayed in Vancouver at Sylvia Court on English Bay, visiting old Yukon friends. I was still dazzled by the wonders of the Outside world: the Bapco Paint sign on the Granville Street bridge, with a mechanical man painting in different colours; a new confection called a Popsicle; the Chute-the-Chute at Hastings Amusement Park; a movie called *Skippy* starring Jackie

Cooper; and a sing-song at the beach sponsored by the Vancouver *Sun* where a strapping girl my own age wrestled me to the sand and asked a curious question: "Has your father got a job?" Of course my father had a job. Didn't everyone's? I was vaguely aware of the Depression; men came almost daily to the back door of my aunt's home in Toronto begging for food; but that had nothing to do with me. It was unthinkable that my father should have no job.

But when he brought the *Bluenose* into Dawson, he found that he, too, was jobless and his world was shattered. The civil service was cutting back; he was being "superannuated," as they called it, before his time on a pension of forty-eight dollars a month. That meant goodbye to the Yukon, goodbye to the *Bluenose,* goodbye to the dog, goodbye to the lazy days on the river, goodbye to the picnics in the hills, goodbye to friends of long standing and goodbye to the good life. Suddenly, every penny counted; we could not afford to bring more than a few prized possessions out of the country with us to our new home in Victoria. When we left at the end of the summer, we left the house we had lived in just as the miners left their cabins, almost fully furnished, new addition and all. My father got seven hundred dollars for that house, which was about what he had paid for it a decade before. There is never a housing shortage in a ghost town.

We have drifted past Hogan's Rock and Wolf Bar and Five Mile Bend and Seven Mile Bend and now, on our right, the log roofs of another dead community can be seen above the blazing fireweed. This is Little Salmon Station at the mouth of the river of the same name, a native village emptied many years before by the scourge of influenza. Flu to an

Indian is as serious as smallpox to a white man. When I returned to the Yukon for that bittersweet summer of 1932, I found that half of my half-breed schoolmates had died of influenza. It was the only communicable disease we knew in the isolation of the North. I did not catch measles, scarlet fever, chicken pox or mumps until I left the Yukon. But for the half-breed children, who made up half the population of our school, influenza was far deadlier than these childhood ailments. All of them had white fathers and Indian mothers. In the winter they lived at St. Paul's Anglican Hostel in Dawson; in the summer they returned to the bush. The previous fall I had been playing with a boy named David Watt on a raft we made in the slough that ran behind the Hostel. When I returned, he was gone. I could not comprehend it; I had had my share of flu and I had not thought of Dave Watt as being any different from me, but it had killed him.

In Little Salmon, the graves are as numerous as the cabins. Indeed, they are like small cabins—a village of spirit houses with sloping roofs, glass windows and curtains, containing dead flowers and teapots and plates for the use of the deceased. That is the way the Yukon Indians bury their dead—or, at least, it is the way they used to.

In the grasses, Patsie finds a pair of sunglasses, which helps make up for the sweater she left behind at the last stop. "You lose some, you gain some," she philosophizes in the log. Peter calls her Sarah Scrounger but no one is surprised any longer to discover such things along the river. At one spot Janet came upon a package of pipe cleaners and tried to use them to tie up the plastic bags but they were so old the wire inside had rusted away.

Carmacks is forty-two miles downstream. To reach it in time to gas up before nightfall, we must use our motors.

A few miles above the settlement we spot, high on the right bank, the old coal mine that George Carmack discovered and worked in the days before he made the famous gold find on Bonanza creek. The only coal in Dawson used to come from this mine and soft, dirty coal it was. We have plenty of time to contemplate the mine because, at this point, The Pig runs out of gas. We hook all the boats together and take turns using one motor at a time. And so we chug slowly into the settlement, singing *Alouette* at the top of our voices.

Above us is the bridge built to carry the new highway across the river. Because of this obstacle no steamboat can navigate the river between Whitehorse and Dawson; a myopic government has allowed the bridge engineers to design a low span without hinge or swing. This is deplorable because the day is surely coming when it will again be practical to run a steamboat excursion on this waterway: there is nothing in the world to match it and the search for new adventures and sensations in a leisure society has only begun. It is difficult to describe the special quality of a Yukon steamboat journey. For one thing, there are the sounds, all of them unique and now obsolete: the steady slap of the paddlewheel against the churning waters; the chuff-chuff of the engine itself, like a great beast panting in its sleep; the regular rumble of each hand cart loaded with birchwood being flung into the belly of the boat as the boiler gang heaved it into the furnaces; and the sharp toot of the whistle greeting the lonely men, waving from the forested banks. From the deck, to use a phrase of my mother's, the long scroll of the forest unrolled hour after hour, seen from a different vantage point than from a canoe. The passengers were three storeys above the water and thus had a kind of bird's eye view of the surrounding landscape. It was always an unhurried trip, the schedule depending upon the moods of the river itself. In midsummer, it was sometimes possible to make the downstream journey from Whitehorse in two days; in the late fall, the struggle upstream could take a week. One was never sure of the schedule and so one never worried; one accepted delays with a certain fatalism and indeed a certain gratitude. Because of its appetite for cordwood the steamboat stopped every few hours at woodcamps located along the river and then we all got off, stretched our legs, picked wild flowers, lay in the sun, and waited for the whistle to sound. Not all of this ritual can be repeated since modern boats would undoubtedly use diesel fuel; yet I can foresee the day when some entrepreneur will want to reproduce those old-style journeys. When he does there will be plenty of willing customers – but not until the bridge at Carmacks is replaced by something more flexible.

We bring the boats into a little beach on our left just beyond the bridge. Skip and his crew head into the settlement to arrange for gasoline and some of the others walk up the dusty road to the local tavern for a cold beer. My nephew finds a pay telephone to relay his latest dispatch to his newspaper. There is not a great deal to see at Carmacks. The town is named for the discoverer of the Klondike's gold, who ran a small trading post on this spot before the stampede. But the settlement that grew up around it, the last remaining centre of civilization between Whitehorse and Dawson, has long since turned its back on the river. Today it faces the new artery of the territory: the highway. Once it was a typical river town: cabins, church, mission house, trading post, school, all constructed of logs, laid out in a neat row on the high bank. Now it is a hodge podge: tavern, gas station, motel, snack bar, grocery store. Carmacks has become a truck stop.

When we return to the boats, the sun, blood red, is low on

91

the horizon. Beside us, three Indians are pulling in their net, silhouetted against the glittering waters. The three big salmon they have trapped are as crimson as the sunset.

I find the odyssey of these Yukon river salmon almost miraculous. For the entire length of the river, they force their way upstream, battling the stiff current, seeking out the exact spot where they were born so that before they die they may reproduce their likeness. In the smaller streams of British Columbia the mystery of the salmon's homecoming is baffling enough, but here it is eerie. These great fish, wriggling in the nets, have been swimming against the full force of the river for two thousand miles, obsessed as no other fish or beast or fowl is obsessed by a craving to return home. So strong is this instinct that they stop at nothing to reach their goal, leaping over obstacles, fighting rapids and shallows and eating nothing until, battered and exhausted, they find that one particular stream where they were raised. That is why the salmon must be netted along the Yukon, or scooped up in a fishwheel, driven by the current; they will not pause to take a fly. Before the white man, the Indian culture was a product of the salmon run and today, sensibly, the law prevents anybody but Indians from taking them. We buy a freshly frozen salmon at the Carmacks store and load it into the freight canoe along with the new supply of gasoline. Then just before we push off, one of the Indians walks over to us.

"Be careful at Five Fingers," he says. "Don't forget to use the right-hand channel."

"I know," I tell him. "The old steamboat channel."

"That's right. The steamboat channel. Keep to the right."

And then he adds, as if by an afterthought: "I lost my father in Five Fingers. Many years ago. He took the other channel."

We thank him and, as the sun turns the waters golden, head down the river, out of range of the Carmacks pollution, and pitch our tents among the tall aspens on a sandy bank above the water. Tomorrow we face the only real obstacle on the upper Yukon – the famous Five Finger Rapids.

The menu calls for corned beef hash and this is my specialty. I soak several packages of dried onions and potatoes until they are soft and crumble in three or four tins of bully beef. I add a couple of eggs, newly purchased in Carmacks, a few dashes of Worcestershire sauce, a chopped clove of garlic and some salt and pepper. Then I sift in a little flour to bind the mixture. In the heavy pan, the bacon grease saved from this morning's breakfast is already sizzling. I form the mixture into patties the size of hamburgers and slide them into the pan. On top of each patty I sprinkle some dried English mustard and spread it around as the patty cooks. Then I flip it over and apply the mustard to the other side. Besides adding a certain tang, the mustard helps the patties to crisp so that when you devour them there is a hot outer crust that crunches under the teeth. Like the salmon, I am also going home; but unlike them, I have no intention of fasting all the way.

DAY SEVEN

This morning we are to face Five Finger Rapids. They lie just around the first bend in the river downstream from our camp and they have been the main subject of discussion during breakfast. My father scarcely mentioned them in his 1898 diary. "Shipped about three bucketsful of water in Five Fingers but none in Rink," he wrote laconically. Like everybody else he kept to the right-hand channel.

In the old days the steamboats on the downstream run used to slip through this channel and over the ledge of rock in a few moments, but the struggle upriver, especially in low water, was a different matter. It took hours to winch the boat through, a tedious experience for the captain though a genuine adventure for the passengers. Sometimes, struggling against the ten-mile current, the boat scarcely seemed to be making any headway and we would spend the day out on the deck, with the boat caught in the racing waters and the rocks towering on either side.

For me, as a boy of five, the rapids were as wonderful an experience as the Chute the Chute. We catapulted through at locomotive speed, my father steering with the paddle and my mother clutching both her children grimly for fear we might topple into the foam. Then, as soon as we were into the calm, I asked my father if we could go back and do it again.

Now, as we drift past more seams of coal, the rapids come into view. Here the river is caught between two cliffs, its passage apparently barred by a wall of broken rock. Through this barrier, the water has torn five narrow channels or "fingers." The rock itself is a conglomerate, composed of various small shales, forced together like bricks by the pressure of time. These four rocky pinnacles, jagged and misshapen, are rendered more grotesque by trees and shrubs that grow out in several directions. Between and around these flower pot islands, the water races savagely. We can see the foam and the spray and hear the river roaring as we approach. To the right, above the steamboat channel, is the remains of the old winching house, long in disuse.

"Whaddya say we take a chance on the fun channel on the left?" Skip suggests. "The water's high enough and it's not really all that dangerous."

In the interests of adventure, we agree to ignore the safe channel and attempt the risky one.

"We'll try it without motors," Skip says. "Keep well closed up."

Robert and Penny are with me in The Slush Box, both making pictures, Penny with the movie camera and Robert taking color stills for a magazine article. They take the stern seat, next to the motor, so they can photograph all of our boat and Skip's boat ahead and then swivel around to show The Pig following behind.

We drift faster and faster towards the frothing channel that squeezes between the two pinnacles of rock on the left. A moment later we are into it, the boat bucking, the spray lashing our faces. I paddle fiercely but I can't hold our boat on course. The current is driving us straight at the great rock on our left.

Patsie, in the lead boat, describes in the log what happens next:

"We started floating down, manoeuvring our craft with paddles, Skip and me in the front. Skip realizes it's not as easy as he thinks. A second of panic flashes across his face, tension mounts, we drop the paddles and he hollers: 'USE THE MOTORS!' *Arg!* We thought we were 'cruisin' for a bruisin',' as we swiftly but definitely began to near the huge, gouged rocks, jutting from the centre of the rapids. Mummy, I'm sure, thought it was her last stand, her face racked with fear. . . ."

In our boat, Robert hears Skip's cry, drops his camera and begins pulling on the cord. More panic! The motor coughs, then dies. The lead boat now has its motor going and has veered off the approaching rocks but we are headed directly for them. The Pig is under power, too, and is swinging over to the right. Just before we strike the rock Robert yanks again on the motor and it sputters to life. He brings The Slush Box hard to starboard and we slip past the jagged edges and under the overhang. And all this time Penny, calmly filming the entire scene, does not take her eyes from the viewfinder.

A few minutes later we are in smoother water and everybody is laughing with relief and shouting from boat to boat. Now nothing will do but that we go back and make the run again under power on the excuse that Robert has not got his pictures. And when that is done (I think again of the Chute the Chute at Hastings Park), we explore the steamboat channel, remarkably tame by comparison. Then we head off towards Rink Rapids, three miles farther downstream.

It is blistering hot. On our left is a little slough, the kind I remember from my childhood, a tree-lined backwater, calm as a farm pond, stretching between two sandy islands. We beach the boats and several of our party fling off their clothes and leap into the water. Thus refreshed we move on through

Rink Rapids, which give us no trouble at all, and pause for lunch at a sandy spit. Some Indian children come down from the forest behind and watch us solemnly and silently and then, as we push off again, vanish into the bush.

Above us, about a foot beneath the topsoil of the bank, erosion has uncovered a white smear, identified romantically on the steamboat charts as Sam McGee's Ashes. This is a layer of volcanic ash, perhaps a foot deep, which runs for many miles through the great valley of the Yukon. Centuries ago, this whole section of the Territory was smothered in ash from what must have been an awesome volcanic explosion. We have been following this line of ash since early the previous morning; its length and thickness indicates the immensity of the eruption that produced it. Other evidence of volcanic activity can be found throughout the northwest: the pitted little black stones mingling with the whiter gravel on the river bars; the hot springs at Takhini and on the Liard and the Toad rivers; the smokey soil at Whitehorse, which makes cultivation so difficult; the telltale cone shapes of some of the mountains; the ash-like consistency of the White river, and in Alaska the famous Valley of Ten Thousand Smokes and the festering volcanoes that glow redly from the islands of the Aleutian chain. Ages ago, when the river was young and these great valleys did not exist, this must have been an unstable land, forever tilting, heaving and rumbling; for that, of course, is how the gold first came, boiling up molten from the earth's bowels only to be ground into nuggets and dust by the abrasive action of blowing sand, shifting ice and running water. It is these same successive tiltings that have produced the wonder of the Yukon Valley, where the benchland drops off in successive steps so that looking up at the hills through half-closed eyes, one seems to be gazing on a series of gigantic terraces.

Yukon Crossing is only a few miles downriver and we intend to look it over. It is Skip Burns' habit to stop and if possible to camp at every historic site along the route. A true romantic, he first visited Alaska with the United States Coast Guard, took his discharge in Skagway, and never left the North. He is enthralled by the history of the Yukon and though he has been down the river numberless times it is always for him a new adventure. He would like to have lived in the Victorian Age of exploration and he bitterly regrets having been born too late to take part in the gold-rush. He sees these little ghost towns not as huddles of ruined cabins but as living communities. He would like to open a roadhouse for travellers at Fort Selkirk, the biggest ghost town of all, and run it in the style of 1898, with bunk beds and a bar serving hootchinoo and red eye and Forty Rod. Another of Skip's dreams is to run a steamboat on the river. Such coarse manifestations of civilization as the garbage dump at Whitehorse and the bridge at Carmacks enrage him and he lives in terror that the money to restore some of the relics of the days of '98 may be raised too late to be of any practical use.

One of these relics is the old roadhouse at Yukon Crossing, so named because it was here that the winter road from Dawson crossed the frozen river. We have reached the half-way point: Whitehorse is 236 miles behind us, Dawson 224 miles ahead. It was in this crumbling inn, then a handsome two-storey log building, that my mother stayed in 1910 on a winter trip back from the Outside. Here the stage stopped for a change of horses and the half-frozen passengers, forced to sit in the open sleigh for the entire journey, tumbled out of the open sleigh for a hot meal and a sleep. My mother has described the mountains of steaming clothing hanging above the pot-bellied stove to dry and the conditions of the journey itself, and our elder children, who heard her tell the story more than once when she was alive, are entranced by this little bit of family history. "It was actually one of the neatest old places we've seen and I wish I could have stayed longer to paint there," Patsie writes in the log. "There was a huge piney wood mountain in the back of the old crumbling lodge, and the lodge was really run down and sunken into the ground." Pamela, who has an eye for such things, finds some original strips of wallpaper still hanging in one of the rooms and gives them to Patsie who attaches them in the proper place in the logbook with Scotch tape. Peggy Anne finds a little slough behind the settlement and, when nobody is looking, goes in for a quick swim. On the bank, Berton comes across a pair of rubber boots, new and exactly his size, which he appropriates. He has forgotten to bring any along and his feet have been perpetually wet.

We expect to make Fort Selkirk by evening, and are planning to spend two nights there to give everybody a free day to relax, clean up and explore the most interesting of the old river towns. At Selkirk, I inform the assembly, we will organize a big campfire, at which everyone must perform. There is a chorus of spurious complaints:

"Aw, Dad, come on! Do we have to?"

But almost immediately there is a great deal of whispering and giggling and plotting as the party breaks up into individual theatrical groups. As we float off down the river again, I notice Cheri and Penny in our boat with their heads together and behind me, in The Pig, I see Patsie and the Deaners chuckling away in secret and I sense we are going to have a memorable campfire.

Soon we have to turn the motors on, since we have a fair distance to cover if we are to reach Selkirk by sundown and there are many sights still ahead on this changeable river.

First, we must cross the Minto Flats, where the Yukon splays out into a broad labyrinth of islands—more than thirty of them in a two-mile stretch—just upriver from Hardluck Slough. The name of the first Governor General to visit the North is commemorated throughout the Yukon. Besides the Flats, there is a Minto Hill, a Minto Bluff and a ghost town named Minto Station; and in Dawson the little park with the World War One obelisk at its centre is called Minto Park. In my childhood, a quarter-century after the vice-regal visit, they were still talking about the event, for the Governor General was a stand-in for royalty and in those days royalty inspired more awe than it does today. Certainly my father was every inch a royalist. He often talked about the time in Banff when he photographed the Prince of Wales making his first post-war visit. He had the photograph to prove it, a treasured possession. He used an autographic camera, which meant that you could actually write on the photograph through a little door at the back, using a special stylus; and on this photograph, he had printed, in his neat draughts-man's hand: HIS ROYAL HIGHNESS AT BANFF. My father, of course, developed and printed his own pictures and some-times in the summertime he would demonstrate the principle of photographic paper by placing a leaf upon a sheet and leaving it out in the sun until the paper darkened, leaving behind the white silhouette with the veins showing lightly. I still have many of the photographs he took with that camera and when I take them out and look at them I can usually remember what was happening on the day they were made. There is a photograph of my sister and me playing on a gravel beach beside the Yukon, and another of my mother in her parka on a winter outing, with her husky dog, Grey Cloud, in the middle of the frozen river. There is a photo-graph of our house taken after my father added the new

100

room, the whole building all but smothered in the canary vine he planted each spring. (I remember he used to measure carefully the monthly rate of the vine's growth.) And there is a photograph of me playing with my own husky, Spark, a present on my sixth birthday. My mother wanted me to give him the more romantic name of Rosy Dawn but I preferred to call him after the horse in *Barney Google*. The strip arrived once a month in a fat parcel of funnies which my grandfather insisted on sending to me over the weak protests of my parents, who thought they were bad for growing boys. It was only years later that I discovered that my father was a devotee of the funnies, too, and that his favorite character was Alley Oop.

And so we enter the regally named Minto Flats, which are marked on the steamboat charts with the warning: "Subject To Change." In sections like this, where the river widens, the channels are never quite the same from year to year. It was like that above Dawson where we used to camp in the summers. Islands would vanish, reappear, change shape, grow larger, diminish or join onto others, all depending on the vagaries of the weather, the current and the season. Familiar spots, where we had once camped on the sand could not always be found the following season. Pools in which we paddled dried up or overflowed. On the charts, the steamboat channel is shown running straight down the middle of the Minto Flats, but it could not have been easy for the pilots to follow.

We stop briefly at Minto Station – more crumbling cabins, including a telegraph post – and I think of Service's line in his verse about the telegraph operator: *Oh, God, it's hell to be alone, alone, alone!* In our trip down the river in 1926 we had stopped at more than one of these solitary telegraph stations whose operators were always fanatically overjoyed to see us. They were all a little eccentric, I thought, and in retrospect, fitted Service's description: *I will not wash my face/I will not brush my hair/I "pig" about the place/ There's nobody to care.* There are no longer any telegraph posts along the Yukon; they have been replaced by radar stations on the highway.

We chug on past Minto Station, past the old stage road which can be seen running through the woods on the top of the bank on our right, past Beef Cache and Devil's Crossing and the site of another abandoned woodcamp, until we approach Hell's Gate Slough and the remarkable rock pallisade that crowns the bank for five miles on our left, broken by a dark fissure bearing the not very original name of Hell's Gate. Selkirk is only ten miles downstream and we reach it around eight o'clock. The sun's low rays turn the long line of buildings on the bank into silhouettes so that the ravages of time are hidden and the town seems to be breathing. But this is illusion. There are no sounds of bells from the church, no howls of husky dogs to answer the steamboat's whistle, no crowds of people jamming the bank, as there used to be when a boat steamed into view. Whenever I think of Selkirk I think of those crowds: the Indian women in their bright skirts and kerchiefs, waving from the bank, the children scrambling about in the dust, the clergymen and priests hurrying down from the missions, the traders standing in the doorways, the police in their dress scarlet posing for the tourists and the dogs, dozens of them, scampering about and howling. Selkirk looks beautifully preserved, especially in the half light of this August evening, but the silence of the graveyard hangs over it.

And then, as we touch into the bank, we notice two canoes parked in the shadows and, looking above us, we see a family of five preparing supper. "Oh, Lord!" says Patsie.

"People!" These are the first river travellers we have encountered in more than two hundred miles and it is as if a spell has been broken. Until this moment, the river has been ours and ours alone. We have been able to stop anywhere, picnic anywhere, pitch our tents anywhere without fear of intrusion. After the fevered campgrounds of the Outside, where the tents and trailers are lined up like suburban bungalows, the Yukon has been a separate world; it is almost as if we had moved back in time to an era before man walked the earth—except that the signs of man have been everywhere. Now man has appeared once more and chosen the best campfire position, too. I can see the annoyance on the younger children's faces.

"Look," says Janet, sternly. "They're probably just as unhappy to see us turning up here in our four great boats with all our equipment and all you complaining kids, as you are to see them."

She climbs the bank to greet them with the same warm, friendly smile I first saw thirty-three years ago on my first day on the campus of the University of British Columbia. I thought then, foolishly, that the smile was especially for me but I soon learned that she smiled that way on everyone. King or peasant, movie star or dead beat, all are treated with identical good humour, for she is a woman without guile or snobbery. She would greet the Prince of Wales or a skid row alcoholic in exactly the same cheerful fashion without either deferring or condescending and if she had a sandwich in her hand or a bar of chocolate she would offer each a bite of it. So now she climbs the bank and walks over to the woman at the top—a handsome woman in her thirties—and exchanges greetings.

The strangers are from New Jersey. He is the vice-president of a big Manhattan bank and both are ardent campers. With their three young children they have brought their canoes down the Teslin river in order to avoid White-horse, since they are trying to escape the blight of civilization, too. They explain that they go camping every summer to some interesting corner of the continent. When Janet asks them why they chose the Yukon, they tell her it is all because of a book they read last winter, a book about the great stampede. Janet, with an enormous chuckle, points down at me, struggling up the bank with a large kitbag, and tells them I wrote it.

The salmon we bought at Carmacks has thawed and we decide to bake it for supper. The fish is easily filleted and cut into fifteen pieces, for Patsie, too, has decided she will break her habit this one time. Each piece is wrapped separately in aluminum foil and placed on an iron griddle on top of the hot coals. Janet includes a little sauce made up of lemon juice, dried onions, celery leaves and soup vegetables (all pre-soaked) together with a little tarragon, salt and pepper.

It is a memorable meal. Nobody is in a rush because tomorrow we can all sleep in. We start with a punch made from lemon and orange crystals and navy rum. Then there are mugs of chicken soup, spiced up by Janet from her supply of condiments. The salmon is fragrant and juicy in its foil wrapping. With it, we eat potatoes, baked in their skins, tinned tomatoes and freeze-dried green peas. For dessert we have bowls of apricots and sweet biscuits. The coffee is made from a dark European roast in a granite pot, with ice cold water from a nearby creek brought to a boil and then removed instantly from the fire.

It is Perri's birthday and our neighbours arrive at the end of our meal with a real birthday cake—a strawberry short-cake, actually baked in a portable reflector oven—complete with one large white candle in the centre. (These people, I think, are even better equipped than we are.) Perri's face glows with gratitude. She is eight today and my mind goes back seven years and five months to the morning when we picked her up from the Children's Aid in Toronto. The whole family assembled for this ceremony and Peggy Anne, the youngest, was chosen to go down the hall with the social worker and bring back the new baby. Thus Perri became Peggy Anne's baby, a gift that prevented any chance of jealousy. Back up the hall she came, holding on to the skirt of the social worker, in whose arms reposed a small, dark bundle. The little head poked out from a swaddling shawl and, beneath an enormous mop of curly black hair, two huge brown eyes regarded us with a mixture of curiosity and suspicion. But now on her eighth birthday, she is very much a Berton and a Deaner to boot.

We invite our neighbours to join us at the campfire. Danny Roberts, the Yukon Indian who acts as caretaker for the ghost town, is invited too, with his wife and daughter. Another boat slips in with a lone male occupant. "The rest of the party decided to stay in Whitehorse," he tells us, "but I was damned if I was going to do that, so I came on alone."

I make a jugful of hot rum and the campfire program suggested this morning begins with songs. The performances that follow are better than I have a right to expect in view of the hasty preparations. Penny has planned an imaginative rendering of an old ballad called "Johnny Verbeck," about a butcher who invents a sausage machine to grind up his neighbours' cats and dogs and is accidentally ground up himself. She has assembled a large cast of the elder children, wearing, alternately, dark jeans and long white underwear so that when they lie down and kick their legs they form the black and white keys of a piano. While the song is being sung by the owners of the legs, Perri, with great aplomb, acts as pianist. Some of the audience think that the piano is supposed to represent Johnny Verbeck's sausage machine but this only enhances the effect. Then Patsie, who has been rehearsing her own group, gives a spirited rendition of Lear's "The Owl and the Pussycat." In an inspired piece of casting Paul takes the falsetto role of Pussycat while Peggy Anne, in a low bass, plays the Owl. Again, Perri is an enormous hit in successive roles as Bong Tree, Piggy Wig and Turkey and when the two leading characters dance by the light of the moon to a slow waltz, Perri suddenly breaks into "Zowie Wowie Baby!" and the audience breaks up. Next, Peter and Berton perform a kind of double monologue in which they pretend to be a couple of Wows making rude comments in hippie talk about our group. Nobody is spared, including the newcomers and the Danny Roberts family – an inclusion which hugely pleases them. And then, after several campfire songs I perform what Patsie describes in the log as my "usual superb spellbinding act of Dan McGrew."

We have saved Skip Burns for the last since he has promised to tell several ghost stories, all of which he swears are true. He is a born performer and within minutes he has most of the audience believing that the eerie incidents, which he insists he has actually witnessed, really did happen. I steal a look at Peggy Anne, leaning forward on her log. Her blue eyes – the only blue eyes in this generation of Bertons (my father's eyes were the same blue) – are wide with wonder and I can see that, as usual, she is both fascinated and repelled, as she is by all stories about witches, werewolves, vampires and other creatures of the night. She loves to be terrified. Watching her now, with the fire flickering on her round eager face, the solemn backdrop of the forest just behind us and the broad ribbon of the river below us, bright under the rising moon, I think of other campfires in other times and my own spellbound terror of things that lurked just behind the dark curtain of the evergreens. It was not spirits that I feared in the Yukon, nor vampires or monsters, for I had never heard of Frankenstein or Count Dracula. Not even that authentic northern ghost, The Walker of the Snows, the silent hunter who leaves no footprints in the snow, sent more than a mild chill up my spine. I feared something much more real and easily comprehended; I feared the wolves with their red eyes and their white, sharp teeth. In my imagination I could see them padding stealthily through the underbrush, waiting to pounce and drag me off. The fear was real because the wolves were real. At night, when my parents were out at an auction bridge party, I could hear the wolves howling in the hills above Dawson. There was nothing between our house and those hills, neither moat nor palisade. The forests drifted on, almost forever, to the very rim of the Arctic, and I imagined them to be full of wolves. In the Carnegie library I had read many stories of these animals and none was calculated to allay my terror. Some were tales of the Canadian north by such writers as James Oliver Curwood, all about lonely trappers, huddling in front of a dying fire, while the encircling ring of wolves closed in. Others were set in Russia where wolves were said to chase sleighs loaded with kulaks who tossed out their children, one by one, to appease the beasts. No wonder when the wolves howled in the hills, the skin on my backbone prickled. Once, on one of the islands in the river, my father showed me the fresh track of a wolf—an enormously long paw print—and the idea that the animal had actually passed that way, perhaps minutes before, and might be even now lurking in the underbrush, drove me into an inner panic. But my most dreadful memory goes back before the days when I could read, to a summer afternoon when we took a picnic to the hills above our home. We had spread a cloth on the ground and were unwrapping the sandwiches when my father decided to walk over to Thomas Gulch, a small ravine nearby, to get a pail of water. I came with him, but the gulch was steep and he told me to wait at the top while he made his way down to the stream. That wait seemed interminable. Suddenly, I was surrounded by the terrible silence of the North—"the silence you most can hear," as Service calls it—no sound at all, save the rattling of the aspens. I called for my father but there was no answering call. For all I knew he had been devoured by a wolf. I called again: silence. The forest began to press in on me and for the first time in my life I felt all alone and lost in the immensity of the wilderness. I began to run, sobbing aloud and repeating over and over again the lines of The Lord's Prayer. I felt the Lord had answered me for I came upon an old cart track in the mosses and this comforting symbol of man's presence urged me on. Then—it must have been only a few minutes later but it seemed forever—I burst into a clearing and there were my mother and my sister laying out the picnic. I felt an enormous wave of relief. "I was lost!" I panted. *"Lost!"* Neither of them seemed to take any notice. A moment later my father appeared with the pail of water. "Why did you come back ahead of me?" he asked and I said nothing because I was ashamed to show my fear. But for many years after that I could not erase the horror of that afternoon from my mind.

Skip finishes his last tale and then, with a howl, he pounces upon Peggy Anne who screams in terror and delight. None of the family wants Peggy Anne in their tent tonight because we all know that after a horror movie or a ghost story she stays awake most of the night. At last, it is agreed that she will stay with Janet and me. By now it is everybody's bed time; Perri has already dropped off to sleep on her log, her face for once in repose and her stomach full of birthday cake. We make our way through the gloom to our beds and the visitors move off to theirs and I look past the orange triangle of my own tent, pitched in the lee of the abandoned Anglican church, and gaze at the hazy contours of the forest, where the white limbs of the birches stand out in the murk like dead men's bones, and I utter a silent thank you that the wolves, at least, are not howling on this night.

DAY EIGHT

Nobody shouts "rise and shine" this morning, because nobody is going anywhere. The sun is already high in a cloudless sky when the first risers tumble from their sleeping bags.

The view from the bank where we prepare breakfast is breathtaking. Spread out before us in a huge semi-circle is the river; beyond it runs a continuous cliff of black basalt. Directly across from us, the Pelly cuts through the wall and mingles its muddy waters with the mainstream. Behind us, the empty village stretches for more than half a mile along the bank.

Selkirk is the oldest settlement on the river. On an island, across from us, is the site of the old Hudson's Bay post that Robert Campbell established in 1848 and fled four years later as the Chilkats from the coast burned it to the ground. Campbell then made a record-breaking snowshoe journey, three thousand miles from this point to the nearest railhead at Crow Wing, Minnesota—an incredible feat. His company did not return to the confluence of the Pelly and the Yukon but in 1898 the Yukon Field Force, two hundred and three soldiers from the Royal Canadian Rifles, the Royal Canadian Dragoons and the Royal Canadian Artillery, made their headquarters here. Their task was to help the Mounted Police keep the peace and prevent the Territory from falling into the hands of the Americans who were pouring down the river by the tens of thousands. Until the steamboat era ended, Selkirk remained a thriving community.

After breakfast, in groups of twos and threes, we begin to explore the settlement. The Anglican church directly behind our campfire is in almost perfect condition, though empty of pews – the floors still polished, the stained glass windows unshattered. In the Mission School next door, the desks sit in neat rows and the last spelling lesson remains scribbled in chalk on the blackboard. We find a supply cupboard bulging with missionary tracts that date back to 1901. They contain stories of dedicated churchmen bringing the Word to the natives of Africa and Asia; but none appear to have been read.

Patsie, Paul and I walk up the old roadway that runs along the river, poking our noses into the various stores and cabins. The police station and the Taylor and Drury trading post are still marked by the original signs. Farther upstream, the cabins are in greater disrepair, doors hanging from broken hinges, windows smashed, some roofs crushed by the weight of the winters' snows. Here again we find the refuse of settlement: a rusted bedstead poking through a tangle of briar roses and the ungainly skeleton of a barber's chair, half hidden in the foxtails.

At the upstream end of the village we come upon the original parade ground and orderly room of the North West Field Force, newly restored by the army with the sites of the old buildings marked on a large map and a stone cairn commemorating the event. The rest of the village demands this kind of treatment, for it is an authentic historic site, but no funds have been set aside for its preservation.

A sign erected by the army points towards the woods where the soldiers' cemetery has been restored. Here, bordering the pathway, are the wildflowers of my childhood: the sweet scented roses, the small purple gentians, the yellow daisy known as arnica and the evergreen leaves and bright red berries of the Yukon holly or kinni-kinnick. In the grass by a deserted cabin I find what must surely be the very last Yukon crocus of the season, really a pasque flower or anemone, known and loved throughout the territory because it is first to bloom in the spring, often poking its purple head through a melting snowdrift. These flowers and others I know from my father, who collected and mounted two hundred and fifty of them, each identified by its Latin name. I can remember him taking me by the hand through the forest and leaning down into the beds of moss to point out the pink twin-flower, with its tiny double blossoms, or the shooting star, which always lived up to its name. In all of his letters to his mother, beginning at Wrangell on the Alaskan panhandle and continuing through the Chilkoot and the river stops to Dawson, he described the flora along the way and enclosed samples of ferns, grasses and bloom. He was an avid gardener and I can still see my mother on the porch, long after midnight, with the sun burning down from the sky, calling for him to stop his weeding and come in to bed. After we moved to Victoria, when time hung more heavily on his hands and he had searched the Men Wanted columns in vain, he would work for hours in his new garden, constructing small ponds, building stone steps through the rockery, erecting trellises for his roses, grafting new branches onto old trees and weeding the vegetables which were so necessary for a family living on a tiny pension. I did not then share his love of gardening; weeding, for me, was an onerous chore. And yet when I got a home of my own I found myself planting the garden I once swore I would never have—a garden that grew and multiplied, as his had. Before I realized it, I was weeding away furiously each summer, late in the evening as he had done, and poring over seed catalogues each winter, planning new additions to my garden. It must be the blood, I tell myself; in spite of what they say about the influence of environment, the blood, too, is strong.

Paul is tiring, so we do not get as far as the graveyard but turn back to camp. He is tired as much from laughing as he is from the walk. He has been laughing almost continuously since we left the last cabin at some secret joke of his own. He has a strange, internal sense of humour and one hears him, from time to time, repeating words and phrases under his breath that have no meaning to anyone else. His curiosities are philosophical and at night he tries to grapple with concepts that have baffled the greatest minds in history. Ever since he has been able to speak he has tried to imagine what the universe would be like if the stars, the moon, the sun, and all the planets were removed. What, he asks himself, is nothingness? Before the stars spangled the sky, what was there? These are exactly the same questions I asked myself at his age when I lay on the porch of our Dawson home on the warmer summer evenings trying to imagine space without stars. It is enough to make one dizzy and it used to make me very dizzy. It makes Paul dizzy, too. In physique he resembles his maternal grandfather; but this restless kind of abstract curiosity comes from his other grandfather, who went regularly to meetings of the Royal Astronomical Society in Victoria and read Jeans, Eddington and Haldane, and worked algebra problems in the evening for fun and grappled with the subject of the fourth and fifth dimension. Paul will not become a mathematician, like my father, though he may become a philosopher but it is more likely he will become a writer, like his cousin Berton. The signs are there and so, too, is the blood.

Some of the family have gone swimming in the slough that

runs into the river below Selkirk. The water is cold but the sun is so hot it does not matter. The grasses and the shrubbery around the tents are draped in clothing laid out to dry. I go for a walk in the woods and come upon an old wagon trail that leads me around behind the village and into a clearing. Here I find a little church standing all by itself in the forest; it must be the Roman Catholic Mission. I enter and find it in perfect condition, with pews and decorated altar, as if ready for Mass, and the faint scent of incense in the air. The Yukon, in my day, was divided neatly between Catholics and Anglicans but the twain rarely met socially. Even in a town as small as Dawson with a population of about eight hundred, where everybody knew everybody else, we did not really know the Catholic kids. We rarely played with them and seldom visited their homes because they went to a different church and a different school. It was the same with the adults. The people my parents knew were those who shared their pew at St. Paul's. My mother was a regular churchgoer who sang each Sunday morning in the choir. My father went less regularly but when he did he revelled in the ritual for he was high church; he crossed himself when the Deity was mentioned and genuflected before entering the pew, actions that made him more than slightly suspect in a community which considered such manifestations suspiciously close to Popery.

He had a passion for ritual and for the things that ritual stood for: the high church, the Empire, the Royal family, the army and the Conservative party. My mother accepted it all but took it less seriously. After we left the Yukon it used to amuse her to watch my father stiffen up when an officer passed us by on the street; indeed she would sometimes nudge me surreptitiously when that happened. Freed of the necessity to vote for the Conservatives in those Yukon days of political patronage, she began secretly to support the CCF and would take me to political meetings in Victoria. She was, after all, her father's daughter. He had been born and raised a Quaker who, after his conversion to Marxism, never again entered a church and who, time and again, ran for office on the socialist ticket in the certain knowledge that he would be defeated. A good deal of this must have rubbed off on his daughter. Once, when I was a boy of about six, I remember her tucking me in bed and I, thinking about the stars and what the universe was like without them, began to ask her questions about God. She answered as well as she could for a while and then she looked at me in an odd way and said: "You know, it is quite possible that there is no God. No God at all." At those awful words the tears started from my eyes. She was clearly nonplussed but she did not retreat from her premise. Yet in all those years I never heard a religious or a political argument between my parents. They loved each other as much, I think, for what they considered each other's idiosyncrasies as for the ideas they held in common.

And, of course, they had come through a good deal together; good times, adventurous times and bad times—the honeymoon days in the tent, the golden years on the river, and then the total disruption of their lives in the North and the harsher depression years in Victoria. Those early Thirties were not years of unadulterated gloom but they could not have been easy for my parents. With his accumulated pensions my father had less than a thousand dollars a year on which to support a growing family. Thus every single cent counted, and that was galling to a man who had never before given a thought to money, who had scarcely saved a penny and who had been used to purchasing on a whim

115

those curious devices that took his fancy and were generally advertised in the back of the *Scientific American* – bridge chips, for instance, and a table that automatically shuffled cards. Now every expenditure had to be weighed. Day-old bread was purchased because stale bread was a nickel a loaf instead of six cents. Fruit and vegetables were bought at the last moment before Saturday night closing when the grocers sold them off cheaply because they wouldn't keep over the weekend. The wood for our fire we gathered from the beaches; my father constructed a dolly which we used to trundle down Transit Road to McNeill Bay and there he and I would saw the driftwood into stove lengths and haul it home along with the strips of kelp which he had discovered made a first-rate garden fertilizer.

A cent was a useful sum of money in those days; a nickel was enormous. Once my mother and I found eighteen cents on the sidewalk three blocks from our house and it was like coming upon a treasure – an event we talked about for years after. For eighteen cents you could buy a pound of stewing beef and several eggs. When the boys in Grade Eight produced a school newspaper by hectograph I could not buy a copy because it cost a nickel; my mother slowly shook her head and said that it was out of the question even though she knew what it meant to me. I wanted desperately to work on its production and, failing that, to own a copy and pore over it; I already had newspapers in my blood, as her father had.

For my own father, this stringency was confining and frustrating. I remember once he was explaining to me the principle of the hot air balloon. He had discovered somewhere, no doubt in the *Scientific American,* a description of how to make a model out of tissue paper. The problem was that we could not afford tissue paper. One day he beckoned me into the basement and unwrapped a roll of red tissue. He had made a pattern for the balloon sections and wanted me to help him cut them out. "No need to mention this to your mother," he said, quietly. "She'd only worry about the money."

Another episode stands out even more distinctly. In the Caramelcrisp shop on Fort Street he had spotted a device that was new to him—the Silex coffeemakers that soon became standard at every lunch counter. The principle of the vacuum, on which they operated, fascinated him and so did the beauty of the bubbles, reflecting the red of the elements, rising in the glass bowls. The following day he took me down to see the wonderful coffeemakers in action and I can remember standing outside in the cold, looking in the windows, waiting for one of the Silexes to empty so we could see the process from the beginning. We waited for a long time until my father said: "You know, boy, I think it's worthwhile going inside and buying a cup of coffee just to watch that thing." It gave me a good feeling because my father called me "boy" only when he felt close to me and it made me feel close to him, too. So we went inside the Caramelcrisp shop and he sipped his coffee very slowly, waiting for the scarlet bubbles to rise in the Silex and when they did, he explained again, carefully, the scientific principle on which the coffeemaker operated. And then he said: "I don't think there's any point telling your mother about that cup of coffee. You know how she is about money."

He could not find work. Young men could not find work and he was approaching 65. Once, at Christmastime, he got a job for two weeks as a postman's helper. For months he advertised in the classified section, offering to teach French or mechanical drawing. He finally got one pupil in mechanical drawing. The first lesson was scheduled right in the

117

middle of our first real summer holiday – a week at a cottage on Shawnigan lake. It meant that my father could not join us for the first half of this slim vacation because he was waiting for his new and only pupil to arrive. Yet for a growing boy there were compensations in having a father who was always home. We spent more time in each other's company than most boys were able to spend with their fathers, working on the beach gathering wood or in the garden or camping in bivouacs made of cedar boughs (we could not, of course, afford a tent) or hiking around the lower Island in the summer and sleeping out under the stars. It wasn't quite the same as the Yukon, where you could camp anywhere, but it was much easier than it has since become to find a piece of forest or a clearing in the woods or a spot beside a lake where civilization had not yet intruded.

In the little church in the woods there is no sound. I find that I am walking almost on tiptoe through the old pathway back to the settlement. Beneath my feet I can hear the crunch of the kinni-kinnick berries.

It is mid-afternoon before we finish lunch. Skip suggests we take a couple of the boats and run up the Pelly to visit the only working farm in the Yukon, operated by two brothers named Bradley. Not everybody wants to go; several are already snoring in the shade. But half a dozen of us pile into the boats and, an hour later, pull into a dock below a farmhouse to the unexpected sight of a barnyard with cattle and chickens scurrying about in the dirt and some two hundred acres of waving grain here in the heart of the wilderness.

In my day there were several farms in the Yukon. There was one on the flat benchland above Dawson, with great haystacks in which we children used to romp, and another a few miles upriver on the banks of a little slough called Sunnydale, where we went on picnics, and others on the low, tear-shaped islands downstream from town. Most of these produced hay and oats for the teamsters but some also grew wheat. Now these have all vanished. Though farming is practical in many places, the Yukon is still a territory obsessed by mining and the laws and customs favour the mining interests over everyone else. Yet this farm on the Pelly has been in continuous operation under various owners since 1902. The brothers Bradley have forty head of cattle and grow both oats and wheat successfully.

The farmers greet us and we walk up towards the main lodge through a dense tangle of Oriental and California poppies and tall blue delphiniums, which have sprung up on their own from seedpods dropped the previous fall—clear evidence of the land's fertility. In the old days, Dawson was a fantasy of bloom in the summer; the swampy soil was rich and the sunlight almost endless. Schizanthus and nasturtiums tumbled out of window boxes; monkshood, larkspur and calendulas popped up like weeds; delphiniums and poppies escaped into the grasses so that long after cabins had mouldered away, these flowers appeared freshly each season. We have seen them from time to time in the old river towns, the tall blue spikes marking the outlines of past settlements.

We go into the lodge and one of the brothers produces a jug of cold milk from the ice box, the first fresh milk we have seen since we left the Outside. We fall upon it like castaways. And then the brothers tell us about the oil men who are prospecting this valley without regard to farms.

"You know I had a man from a big American company sitting right here last year in this living room where you're sitting, telling me it was okay to keep farming for another year!" one of the brothers tells us.

My nephew Berton pricks up his ears, sensing a story. The

farmer explains that he and his brother do not own the mineral rights on their land and so, technically, under mining law anybody can stake it for gold or oil or any other mineral.

"Their surveyors had been over it and had staked it but they told us they wouldn't be moving in just yet so it was all right to keep farming. Right in my own living room! We took them to court and had the staking declared illegal. Now what do you think of that?"

We think that long after the minerals have been dredged or pumped from the earth, the soil of the Yukon will still be rich enough to grow oats and if there is no fresh milk in Whitehorse and Dawson it is not because cattle cannot be raised here but simply because of the feeling that this is strictly mining country – a fixed idea that is the legacy of the stampede. We finish our milk and bid the farmers goodbye and set off down the Pelly towards Selkirk, thinking how disappointed the others will be when they hear what we saw and what we had to drink.

Supper is not quite ready and so we lie back on the edge of the bank in the early evening sun, watching the river and the sky. There is a touch of fall already in the air. I notice that the Michaelmas daisies are beginning to show their purple heads above the grasses while in the sky a few mallards and Canada geese are winging south. The mornings are already crisp and before long the tenderer flowers will be blackened by the first frost. August, after all, is an autumn month in the Yukon. Frost usually strikes around the 20th. Indeed, I can recall times when it hit Dawson before Discovery Day, the 17th, ruining the flower and vegetable judging. But generally the weather held past the big day and the cauliflowers from my father's garden, nearly as big as cartwheels, and the marrows, three feet long, and the sweet peas, with as many as seven flowers to a stem, would more often than not win him a blue ribbon. It is difficult to describe the size, texture and flavour of vegetables grown on summer days when the sun shines for twenty-two hours. Our celery, for instance, had a crispness and a nuttiness not found Outside and the cabbages, as big as soccer balls, were firm and crunchy from the heart to the outer leaves.

Pamela announces that the beans she has been working on all day are ready. Beans are a Yukon staple; it is hard to imagine the stampede without them, for in those days they were cooked and frozen and carried like marbles in men's pockets and thawed out in the mouth on the trail. In my boyhood, beans were served at children's parties as sandwiches are served today. Our Wolf Cub hikes in the hills centred around a pot of beans. Each boy was asked to bring a tin of them and all these tins were poured into the common pot and heated up together. But Johnny Gould and his two brothers brought along a brown pot of their own, containing their mother's home baked beans. Sometimes John would throw these into the common pot but more often, it seems to me, the brothers would refuse to taint the best baked beans in town with the tinned variety and would cook and eat their own.

As we clean up the last of our plates with pieces of toast grilled over the flames and the dishwashing crew moves to its task, a cry goes up for more ghost stories. I see Peggy Anne's face light up with fearful expectation and realize that we are again going to have company in our tent. The teenagers are already talking about the cemeteries behind the settlement and about the ghosts living in the silent cabins to our rear. Now, as dusk falls and the fire drops to a mass of coals and the rum is added to the coffee and a sighing little wind springs up to rattle the aspen leaves, I decide to tell them all the legend of the Lost Cabin.

121

"What *is* the Lost Cabin, Dad? I've heard you mention it before."

"It's something we don't talk about too much, Patsie. Like the Walker of the Snows. But there's a song about it, you know."

"A song? Sing it, Dad."

"I'll do the first verse."

I give it to them in a minor key, slow, melancholy and brooding:

Oh, somewhere north of Sixty, where a clump of birch trees bloom
By a valley in the Yukon, there's an old, abandoned flume
On a bleak and lonely hillside, where the trees are white with frost
There's an empty, moss-chinked cabin that is lost . . . lost . . . lost
And many men have sought it to their cost

"Was there *really* a Lost Cabin?" Peggy Anne asks. "Or is it made up? Were there spooks in it?"

So, allowing myself to be persuaded, I tell them the story:

"Somewhere back in the hills on the benchland over-looking an unnamed valley, there is supposed to be an old cabin sitting on one of the greatest claims in the Yukon — a claim, it is said, richer even than Number Sixteen on Eldorado.

"There are some who claim to have seen that cabin, but only in the distance. Generally they were so far gone that they couldn't finish their journey. The odd thing is that almost everybody who claims to have seen it, places it in a different part of the country. There was a half breed who came out of the Upper Pelly country who claimed he'd seen it; but he'd lost a lot of blood from a fight with a grizzly and he didn't know for sure where. Then there was Bert Masters who described the cabin just before he died; they brought him back, raving, from the Nordenskiold country but nobody else could find a trace of it. Charlie MacGurkey always insisted it was on the far side of the Rat River Divide and his description was like all the others: a snakelike valley and a ridge above it with a clump of white birch trees and an old, abandoned flume. MacGurkey saw it in the distance but his grub had run out and, as it was, he scarcely made it back to civilization. Lost three fingers and some of his toes from frostbite and was out of his mind for weeks before he pulled through.

"Anyway it was MacGurkey who offered to go back and find the cabin. He was grubstaked by an outsider named Kronstadt. They took along a third fellow, not much more than a boy, who went by the nickname of Tubby. The three of them set out in June and headed for the Rat River Divide – the same place where Bishop Stringer almost starved to death and was forced to eat his boots and where Inspector Fitzgerald's Mounted Police party died of hunger after eating all their dogs.

"Somewhere along the way, about August, there was an accident, brought on, I think, by an argument. Tubby fell or was pushed off the edge of a cliff and was impaled on a dead tree part-way down. One of the others went down after him but he didn't bring him back up again. You can guess why. The man was badly injured. He would have to be taken back to civilization. That would mean the search for the gold of the Lost Cabin would have to be abandoned. The thing was disguised as an accident but it's pretty clear that Tubby was pushed the rest of the way to his death.

"After that the going grew rougher. MacGurkey and

123

Kronstadt had to go on half rations because the way seemed longer than MacGurkey remembered. They'd climb to the top of a ridge and look out across the valley and there'd be another ridge to climb. It went on like that for weeks and still no sign of what they were seeking.

"There was an early freeze-up that year. By early October the weather turned cold and the first snow began to fall. Still they pushed on, following MacGurkey's memory of his old trail, both of them growing weaker and, I'd guess, more cantankerous along the way.

"By the end of the month they were out of food and lost in a blizzard so bad they couldn't see more than a few feet in front of them. Kronstadt was suffering terribly from frostbite and was hard put to keep up with MacGurkey who was in no mood to wait for him. The white storm increased in fury—the wind howling like a banshee—and they knew that if they didn't keep moving they'd die. They moved on more by an act of will than anything else, following a twisting valley whose outline was barely visible in the storm.

"Suddenly it hit MacGurkey that he'd seen this valley before—the valley that was shaped like a snake—and as this revelation came to him the storm suddenly died and there, high on the ridge above them, he could see a clump of birches as white as dead men's bones and the long line of an old flume, pointing down the valley like a skeleton's finger and, silhouetted against the sky, the dark outline of an old cabin. It was then that he knew they'd found what they were seeking.

"So they began to clamber up the hillside to the bench above. They could see the old diggings, scarring the hill, and the flume, badly in need of repair, which had probably brought water from a lake somewhere back in the hills. The cabin itself was in bad shape with the roof half caved in and the door hanging loosely on one hinge. But at least the storm had abated.

"And so they reached the cabin and grabbed for the door. But as they did it opened, as if by itself, and it was then that they realized the cabin was occupied. An old prospector, his hair as white as snow and his cheeks as pale as death, peered out and greeted them. 'Welcome gentlemen,' he said, 'come on in . . . I've been expecting you. Got some coffee on, just waiting for you to drink it.' And he beckoned them into the cabin and poured out three cups of coffee, which he offered them because, he said, he knew they must be cold. 'Why,' said Kronstadt, 'there's only two of us; you've handed us one cup too many.' 'Oh, no,' said the old man, 'this extra cup is for your friend. Go on, pass it to him. He arrived some time ago—just after the first frost.'

"And there was Tubby, with a ghastly smile on his face and the blood hardly dry on his chest and a piece of dead tree still sticking through him. 'Hello,' he said, 'it took you guys a long time to find the Lost Cabin.' "

Peggy Anne is beside herself. "Is it true? I mean is it *real*? Did it really happen?"

"Well, they claim it did."

"But . . . but," her brow furrows. "If it *really* happened, how did you find out about it—if, like, everyone was dead?"

"Can't say, Peggy Anne; I'm only telling the story the way I heard it."

"Did you ever *see* that cabin?" The odd thing about Peggy Anne is that even when she is serious and feeling weird inside from the story, she can't help smiling.

"Not me. Would I be here if I'd seen it?"

"Sing the song again, Dad," Patsie asks.

"Well, there are several verses. I'll sing the last one."

Oh, each man has his cabin . . . and each man has his dream
And for each man there's a hillside and a flume beside
*   a stream*
And each man seeks his cabin to his last expiring breath
And he finds it on the hillside slopes of death . . . death . . .
*   death*
On the bleak and lonely hillside slopes of death.

Now there is absolute silence around the fire.

"I'll give twenty dollars to anyone who'll sleep in the old graveyard tonight," I say, wickedly.

No one takes me up on the dare. Instead, one by one, they drift off to their tents except for Peggy Anne, who slips into ours.

"It's a hell of a story," Patsie writes in the log, as she describes the events of the day. "Dad had to stare out into space as if he wasn't looking at anyone else because he'd break into laughter."

There is no point in telling any of them, even Patsie, that years ago I made the story up for a radio play and later turned it into a folk ballad for a Toronto revue where it was sung to the accompaniment of a guitar by a promising young performer named Robert Goulet. Nobody in the Yukon has ever heard of the Lost Cabin.

DAY NINE

The day is made for drifting. High above us on the right bank as we push off into the channel we can see the spectacular wall of rock–a sheer cliff of columnar basalt, jet black, rising four hundred and fifty feet to a poplar-topped plateau. This rampart runs from the Pelly's mouth all the way to Twin Falls, some eighteen miles downriver – a great palisade, looking as if it were fashioned by some monstrous hand. On the opposite side the eroded banks rise six feet from island-dotted waters.

Paul suggests that the family stick together and so the three rubber boats and the canoe move into the centre of the channel and are then lashed into one great floating island, rotating slowly in the broad Yukon. From beneath us there comes a familiar rasping sound, which puzzles the children. I explain that it is the silt-laden waters of the Yukon, enriched by the new sand of the Pelly, scouring the sides of the boats like soft sandpaper. This abrasive whisper is one of the sounds of my boyhood and I remember my father explaining it to me as we drifted back home to Dawson one evening in the old *Bluenose*.

The phrase "one big happy family" pops into my mind. At this moment, the cliché describes us exactly as we float through the wilderness. Some of us are reading; others are talking and watching the scenery unwind; the Wows are starting a poker game to Paul's competitive delight; Perri, who has been playing with her doll, sets it aside to comb Cheri's hair; Skip is playing the harmonica; Peggy Anne is drawing pictures and so is Patsie, finishing a sketch of Fort Selkirk in the log book; Penny is weaving a macramé headband for her mother. Both Penny and Pamela make their own Christmas presents—lampshades of tissue paper, scarves of Batik work, dolls and dolls' clothes for the little girls, crocheted and knitted things. Is this part of the so-called new "youth culture," I wonder, or—thinking of my father and his loom—is it, too, in the blood? He picked up the idea of weaving from my Aunt Florrie, my mother's eccentric sister who came from Toronto to live near us in Victoria. She had been an art student like Patsie, and had studied painting on the left bank in Paris. She had a small hand loom on which she used to weave brightly coloured belts and headbands and this caught my father's curiosity. While her interest was artistic, his was scientific. He began with a small loom but soon graduated to more complicated devices. Nothing would satisfy him but that he design and build his own loom, inventing and adding refinements. On this creation he produced, from designs carefully laid out on graph paper, the most beautiful fabrics. Once he wove cloth for a tweed suit for my sister, tailored it himself, and carved all the buttons by hand. He became, of course, an active member of the Weavers Guild for he never entered upon any enterprise without going into it fully. I had thought that the loom was lost but now I learn from Pamela, who is also a weaver, that it is still in the basement of Lucy's home in Vancouver. Pamela says it is in good condition, and that she is having it shipped east where she intends to use it. She adds, not without a sense of challenge, that it is perhaps the most complex loom she has encountered. It must be in the blood, I think.

Suddenly, Janet lets out a cry: "Bears! Over on the right!"

There are two of them, half-way up the hill, looking for berries. In the binoculars I examine the broad face masks and the heavy shoulders: they are grizzlies. It is odd that I should have been more afraid of wolves in my childhood than of the great grizzlies who are much more dangerous. I knew one man who was killed and partly eaten by a grizzly; and on Saltspring Island in British Columbia I met my mother's friend, the famous Jim Christie, who fought a grizzly to the death and was himself so badly mauled he was given up for dead. You could still see the scars on his forehead where the animal had pulled his scalp down over his face before breaking his limbs.

The bears hear us shouting and begin to race up the hill at an amazing speed. No animal that I know moves faster against gravity.

"You might be able to get away from a grizzly going downhill," says Skip, "but if you're running uphill – no way, man, no way!"

The sun grows hotter as we drift into the mid-afternoon. Most of us have sunburns and cracked lips from the reflection off the water. Paul is calling again for "rationale" and Janet passes out a light lunch that she and Pamela have made up. After the usual squabble about the size of the chocolate bars ("too small," "not enough to keep a flea alive," "need a microscope to find them," etc. etc.), Paul suggests that we have a sing-song. Once again we break into the familiar *Alouette*. Then Skip sings *his* favourite: *I Had a Dog Whose Name Was Blue* and Patsie and I oblige with *The Walloping Window Blind*, which I have been teaching her en route. The singing diminishes and finally dies away – an echo lost in the silent hills – as, one by one, the choristers drop off to sleep, pillowing their heads on dunnage bags or sweaters or on the inflated sides of the rubber boats.

Looking on this tranquil scene it occurs to me that this is probably the enduring vision that will return to warm me in later years. More than the memory of the last night's camp-fire, more than the wild moments on the lakes and in the rapids, this sunlit spectacle of the entire family relaxing and drifting will stay etched in my mind. It is very difficult to relish such moments except in retrospect. Generally, when they occur, one does not think of them as particularly significant. Maugham once wrote that he had enjoyed many hours of real romance in various odd corners of the world but he had seldom realized at the instant they happened that they *were* romantic. Ever since reading those lines I have tried to see every day in terms of both the past and the future. One of the devices I use is to pretend, at any given instant, that I am an old man at the close of life thinking back to the days when I was in my prime and longing to relive them. Whenever I play this game the sky at once seems bluer and the grass greener. I am playing it now, lying back in the boat and looking over my family in the guise of an old man who has been given a brief reprieve to re-experience a moment from the past. I see my children, as I see the river, in terms of both the past and the future – as the toddlers they once were and as the adults they will soon become. I think of them as grandparents with children of their own and I wonder again which one of them will be the first to return to the river and whether these successive voyages by the third and fourth generations may become a kind of family tradition (for I have inherited my father's love of ritual). And I wonder again what the river itself will be like a generation hence.

There is another way of looking at moments like this and that is to see them in terms of one's own past. When I want to feel the sun grow warmer I compare whatever I may be doing at the moment with what I was doing at the age of 17 when I worked in a mining camp on Dominion creek, forty-odd miles from Dawson. This, too, is a way of making the sky bluer and the grass greener, for those three seasons on Dominion, especially the first one, were the most gruelling of my life. It was not so much the work, which was hard enough, but the fact that there was no respite. I laboured, ate and slept, then laboured again with nothing to look forward to until the end of the season. I hated the work. The first season I was a carpenter's assistant, helping to build bunkhouses for the mining crew; the next two I toiled on the mud flats as part of the thawing crew. It was not creative and it was not productive; I was doing it solely for the money. Yet my classmates envied me because I had managed to get a summer job.

I went to work on my seventeenth birthday, near a ghost town called Paris, so named because some hundreds of Frenchmen, or perhaps French Canadians, had camped there during the stampede. I knew of it because my father had once taught there in the early days. He spoke French, not because of his Huguenot heritage but because he had taken the trouble to learn the language on his own after he graduated as a civil engineer from the University of New Brunswick. Dominion creek was already familiar ground to him because it was the site of his first stampede in the fall of 1898, shortly after he arrived in Dawson. New ground was said to be opening up and he was one of those who rushed to stake it. "We had a tramp of 45 or 50 miles out and intended to stake it between August 31 and September 1," he wrote to his younger brother Jack, "but on the 31st it poured cats & dogs. I was the only one of our party who had taken a water-proof oiled sheet with me. Wright & I were to stake together and witness each other's stakes, so we were walking together & when the rain got heavy we stopped & rigged up the sheet like a lean-to on 4 stakes, built a fire in front & got underneath it till the rain let up a bit. . . . The night was very dark and we had to stake by the light of wax vestas. . . . When we got back from Dominion after staking, and a rotten trail it was, we went in to try and record; and after trying to get into the Recorder's office for four days we found that that part of the creek on which we staked had never been opened up at all so had all our tramp for nothing. . . ."

So on my seventeenth birthday, by sheer coincidence, I was going to work almost on the very spot where, thirty-nine years before, my father had tried to make his fortune. We were bunked in an old, two-storey log roadhouse that went back to the goldrush days and had few amenities. Often in the mornings, we broke a film of ice to get at the water in the wash-basins. We rose at six, scrubbed our faces, wolfed down an enormous breakfast and walked three miles to work, which began at seven. We worked a ten-hour day, walking back for lunch and supper and by the time supper was over we were all exhausted, or at least I was. There was little to do except to go to bed. My fellow workers were all much older than I was; some were well over 50 and a few were over 60. Almost all were recent immigrants. Sometimes we talked a little before bedtime; I remember the cook telling me that his uncle, who owned a haberdashery in Vienna, had been arrested because he put in his window a tie with a red band, which the authorities identified as a Nazi symbol. I did not know whether to believe him. There was a good deal of argument about the Nazis at the time, especially among the Germans and Austrians—*anschluss* was only a year away—but I paid little attention for I was too weary and the terrible tocsin of the morning triangle sounded at six, every single day, including Sundays and holidays. There were no days off—none. That was the dreadful thing about those summers.

Every day was like every other day. Autumn seemed interminably far away. We were like prisoners in a concentration camp, hoping for release but not really expecting it. And so I worked my seventy hours, week after week, living for the day when the river would take me away to a different world. Sometimes I remember thinking about my future life (for at the time I had no idea what I was going to do with myself) and wondering whether it would always be like this or if a time might come when I would have a job that would allow me to rise at my leisure and drift down to the office or to take real holidays when I could lie on my back and gaze at the sky.

Now, on the river, lying on my back and gazing at the sky, the moment seems sweeter from the contemplation of the past. The river, I notice, has changed again. We have long since passed the basalt wall and now seem to have entered some dark Norwegian fiord, where the mountains rise directly from the water enclosing us on both sides. It is time to start looking about for a camping spot. Because of the mountains and the lack of shoreline, this is not easy. We untie the boats, turn on the motors and speed off down the river, Skip and I in the lead, scanning the shore for a level spot. On our right, on the very edge of the bank, I see a big, tawny tomcat staring at us, only to realize that this wilderness is scarcely the place to encounter a domestic animal. It is, of course, a lynx. He seems to have been struck dumb at the sight of us and it occurs to me that he has probably never before seen a human being. We bring the boats into the shore for a better look and only then does he change from a statue into a moving animal, loping gracefully into the woods like an oversized alley cat.

After several miles, we come upon a low, sandy cove. Here we find wild onions and high bush cranberries in profusion and small puffballs in clusters along the edge of a small swamp, all identified by Pamela, who has made herself an expert on edible wild foods. At home she has boiled up nettles and served them like spinach and made jam from the fruit of the May Apple. Now she bustles about picking the cranberries for she has figured a way to make up for our depleted supply of mixer. She boils the berries, drains off the fluid and blends it with vodka, producing what is known in more sophisticated circles as a Cranbreaker Cocktail. Meanwhile, I send the smaller children to gather hatsful of puffballs. These I fry in a mixture of oil and butter, adding Pamela's wild onions for flavouring. We eat them as hors d'oeuvres and they are delicious, crisp like French fries on the outside and firm and hot in the centre.

Watching Pamela searching for wild and edible things, I think of my father and his two hundred and fifty pressed and mounted flowers, gathered in the hills during his final years in the Yukon in the late thirties, when he had so little to do with his long evenings – no wife, no children and no really close friends.

Why did he think he had to go back? I ask myself, as I have asked myself so many times in the past. The answer has nothing to do with the call of the wild or the spell of the North. Simply, he felt it to be his duty to his family.

The call came in the middle of the Depression. The only other mining recorder in Dawson, his former office partner, suddenly died. Someone was wanted immediately – someone who knew the job; and that someone could only be my father. "Must have Berton," the telegram to Ottawa read, with a copy to my father, who contemplated it with satisfaction. This man, who had been idle for three years and who was now past official retirement age, was being offered his old job back.

Ever since his superannuation he had been bitter about losing his job. He was a war veteran, with two small children and, in his eyes, it was rotten treatment. That was the word he used again and again in his letters of complaint to Ottawa and in his conversations with utter strangers. He insisted on telling everyone the story and at considerable length. It began to embarrass me to hear it. "Is he at it again?" my mother used to say to me and I would nod. "I wish he'd forget it," my mother would say. "I wish he'd forget it, too," I'd reply. For my father, who could be compelling on almost any other subject, was becoming a bore on this one.

There was no argument, then, about his going back. That was assumed. He would go back to the Yukon but we would stay behind. It was too expensive to move again and besides, we children were settled into a new school, joining new social institutions, making new friends and discovering a new world. The Yukon, my father knew, was a wonderful place to raise children; it was not the best environment for teenagers.

But why did he need to go at all? It is true that we had to skimp to make ends meet, but then so did many others and certainly we were not starving. Why wrench himself away from the family he loved—not just for a few months, but for years? Why condemn himself to a solitary existence in a backwater mining town? The answer was that he felt he could not turn down a Job, for in the thirties the concept of Job was holy. At school we were divided into those whose fathers had Jobs and those whose fathers were Jobless. To be offered a Job—especially a Job you knew you could do—and to turn it down for selfish reasons bordered on the heretical. It was his duty to support his family, even if it meant banishment from that family. It was not just the idea of more money—though money in those days was something everybody thought about and talked about—it was the knowledge that without money his children could not be properly educated. My father could not bear the thought that we might not be able to go to university, and yet that awful possibility had been in his mind since we left the Yukon. It did not occur to him that we might get along in life quite easily without a university career. More than anything else, I believe, that was his main reason for returning to the North.

And so he made his preparations to leave us. With the prospect of more money coming in he felt that he and my mother could afford a brief excursion. It was decided that she would accompany him to Vancouver and spend several days there with him before he set off for the North. It had been a long time since the two of them had enjoyed a holiday together and this would be like another honeymoon. The excitement of it all helped to alleviate the wrench of the coming departure. I remember my mother buying a smart burgundy suit with matching hat for the occasion and being quite gay at the prospect of a boat trip to the bigger city.

Then, almost at the last moment, she collapsed from sheer nervous exhaustion. I do not know what the doctor's diagnosis was but she was clearly overwrought and running a high fever. The days slipped by and it soon became clear that she could not go to Vancouver. It was too late anyway. My father could no longer delay his own departure north.

On the day he left, Bob Allen, his old Dawson colleague who had been superannuated at the same time, was waiting in his Model A Ford to take him down to the CPR dock to catch the boat to Vancouver. My father went into my mother's room, sat down beside her on the bed and quietly closed the door and I could hear them talking in low tones for some time until Bob Allen honked his horn. Then the door opened and my father came out and his eyes were red and I could see my mother crying softly into her pillow and I felt that I had never in my life been so miserable.

We helped him with his bags and climbed into the back seat of the car, my sister on one side and I on the other, with our father's arms around our waists. And as Bob drove slowly down Fort Street, my sister began to cry and I had to fight back the tears for, having turned fifteen and now being the man of the house, I was determined not to cry then or ever again. I can remember my father saying, over and over again: "They're good children, Bob; they're good children," and Bob answering: "Yes, they *are* good children, Frank," and then we were at the dock and he was going up the gangplank, waving back at us, and the boat was whistling and he was gone and nothing was ever quite the same again.

"I should never have let him go back," my mother would say sometimes in the years that followed. "Why did I let him go back?" And often over the years I have wondered about cause and effect: how would things have turned out if she had persuaded him to stay in Victoria? On the river of life there are many unexpected twists. If my father had not crossed the Chilkoot and come down the Yukon but had returned instead to the sinecure of a professorship, he would not have met my mother and that particular family would not have existed. If he had not gone back to the Yukon, I most certainly would never have gone to university and thus would not have met my wife and then this family, eating curried chicken here by the fire, would not exist and there would be no Pamela gathering wild things in the forest on the banks of the ever-widening river.

DAY TEN

We are floating once again between the mountains – "the scraggy, sculptured, hardrock mountains," as Patsie describes them – that rise on our right "like eternal bookends, barricading us from the beyond," scarred by moving glaciers, long since melted, that have "bitten and gobbled through the mountainsides."

Soon, on our left, we pass the old settlement of Selwyn (at the mouth of Selwyn creek), where my father and his party stopped in 1898. "Some of the boys," he wrote to his mother at the time, "prospected the creek, which was staked to the source, but was suspected to be 'salted.' Nobody had yet got to bedrock so no one could tell anything for sure about it." My father did not wait to find out and his party did not bother to record their claims; there was no gold found on Selwyn creek, and no gold on any creek where my father drove in his stakes. But then he had not really come to the Yukon for gold, not that first time at any rate; he had come for adventure.

Yet there was a good deal of gold to be discovered along this stretch of the river. Cabins, marking the old settlements, can be seen every few miles and behind these cabins the remains of old roads run back into the forest to abandoned placer diggings.

We stop for lunch at Coffee creek, under the shattered

remnants of a disused trading post and eat our sandwiches amid a tangle of briar roses and raspberry bushes. The berries are our dessert; they are here by the thousands waiting to be eaten, if not by us then by the bears.

But we see no bears on this section of the river, only the ghosts of other times. At Thistle creek, twenty-three miles downstream, there is an abandoned river barge and another two-storey roadhouse, where my mother stayed on that winter's journey back to Dawson after she had made up her mind to return to the Yukon and marry my father. I think of her sitting in that open sleigh between the two old men, swathed in coonskin and wondering whether she was doing the right thing in returning to this remote corner of Canada to marry this curiously attractive but absolutely penniless labourer who taught her French and read Greek and seemed to know so much about the stars and the wildflowers and who thought nothing of hiking into Dawson from Dominion creek – more than forty miles in below zero weather – just to spend an evening with her.

He was a man of seemingly inexhaustible energy and I can still remember the day when I realized for the first time that he was mortal. It was on a Sunday just before my seventeenth birthday – the summer my mother and I returned to the Yukon, she to see my father for the first time since his departure and I to take the job he had arranged for me. We had all changed. My father seemed to have shrunk in stature for I had grown taller and he had grown greyer. My mother's hair had turned pure white; it had always been white, she told me in one of the many moments of intimacy we enjoyed when we were thrown together by my father's exile. She had been dyeing it since she was a young girl, but since dyed hair was not fashionable, she had kept it a secret; now she saw no reason to continue. My father had occupied those intervening years in a variety of ways; he had got himself a small canoe so he could once again enjoy the river and gather his wildflowers. In the winter, he would often go down to the office in his spare time and work, or occupy himself by grinding a concave mirror for a reflecting telescope, a meticulous task that took him more than two years. He showed me how he was doing it and explained the principle of focal length and the difference between a refracting and a reflecting telescope but I cannot say I understood it fully, even when he brought out the diagrams, carefully laid out on his familiar graph paper. The odd thing was that once the mirror was ground to the proper focal length and carefully polished and silvered, he set it aside and did not bother to construct a telescope around it. That was, after all, a mere assembly job; the real challenge had been met. It was the same with the stampede: he sought the gold as a kind of afterthought. In his letters to his mother and his brother, he had remarkably little to say about his search for gold, though he did stake a claim on Quigley Gulch without result. He wrote about the look of the country, the change of the seasons, the shift in temperature (which he noted daily in his pocket diary), the size of the mosquitoes and the exact details of log cabin construction. In one letter, he even included three scale drawings of the cabin he built on Quigley Gulch – a front and rear elevation and a floor plan. He described, in a passage of several paragraphs, the Yukon stove that heated the building and the principle on which it worked; but he had not much to say about the gold fever, which was making headlines in the newspapers Outside.

On this summer Sunday before my seventeenth birthday we set off, the three of us, on a picnic hike along the Klondike river. We had reached the deserted warehouses at Guggieville, named for the Guggenheim Mining Company, when suddenly my father sat down on a rock by the side of the road. I was full of energy and wanted to press on.

"Let's just wait a few minutes," my father said.

"No – let's get going. Come on!"

"You have to understand that your father may be a little tired," my mother said, quietly.

My father tired? I found that hard to comprehend. Only a few years before he and I had hiked for a hundred miles around the southern end of Vancouver Island, up through the Devil's Potholes in the Sooke river and through the reservoir reserve to Shawnigan lake and back by way of Cobble Hill, Brentwood and the Saanich peninsula. In those days it was I who had wanted to sit down and he who had shouldered my pack when it became too heavy. Now our positions were reversed and it came as a shock. It was hard to realize that there were fifty years between us. He had never been a "pal" to me, in the worst sense of that phrase; he had been a father. But he had seemed no older than the fathers of the boys I knew; often he had seemed younger. But now, as he approached seventy, he showed that he was mortal and so we rested that day and took it easy on the road back to town. A few days later I turned seventeen and my mother baked my favourite coconut cake but before I could eat it my name appeared on the company employment sheet. I had just time to get my gear together and rush down to the livery stable to board a truck for Dominion creek, where the dredge crews would soon rip up all the cabins and the wheelbarrows and the tell-tale signs of the goldrush, including those original stakes which my father had helped pound in almost half a century before.

On our left, the mountains have vanished; we are passing open country, flecked with marshes. The mouth of the White river looms up – a great stream, choked, as its name implies,

141

with glacial silt and probably volcanic ash from the Kluane range of mountains. The Yukon, which was once light green and then baby blue and later a rich brown, now turns greyer and the thickening waters become undrinkable. The mouth of the White is blocked by islands formed from the same silt, their wet and colourless flanks encumbered by the bleached trunks and branches of dead trees swept downstream in the high water and left in great heaps on the sandbars. These "snags," as they are called, clog the river for miles below this point, the skeletal branches reaching far out over the water, a menace to small boats, some of which have been caught in their clutches and swamped.

My parents floated through this labyrinth at midnight on that trip down the river in 1926. Though the nights never grow dark in July, that particular evening was gusty with a threatening storm so that a kind of twilight settled on the land. We children, asleep in the bottom of the boat, were awakened with a start. I remember the scene only dimly but the sight of my father's face is still imprinted on my mind; I saw the same look on Skip's face when Scotty signalled with the oar that he was in trouble on Laberge. I looked up from my sleep and saw that we were passing directly beneath an enormous snag, the boney fingers brushing at our boat as we swept under it, my father desperately pushing at it with the paddle. It was a close call—something my parents talked about for many years.

That was near the mouth of the Stewart river, which flows in from the right. Stewart City, or what remains of it, is situated on an island. I cannot recognize it now. In the old days this was a thriving settlement, when the steamer *Keno* pushed barges of silver ore down the Stewart from the mines at Keno Hill, transferring them to the larger boats on the Yukon. Stewart had a Northern Commercial Company store, a post office, a telegraph station, servicing facilities and the usual gaggle of trappers' cabins. Now the river has eaten away half the island and little evidence of the old town remains. The buildings that have survived have been moved well back from the crumbling bank. Stewart's population is down to four – a trapper and his family who run a small store and gasoline cache.

Patsie, the vegetarian and animal lover, is appalled by the sight of furs for sale in the store: "It makes me sick to see them all lined up on the counter," she scribbles angrily into the logbook. I think, a little guiltily, of the superb silver tip grizzly rug in my den at home. I bought it ten years before from my old Dawson schoolmate, Chester Henderson, the grandson of that same Robert Henderson who, with George Carmack, is credited with starting the goldrush. Chester, one of the calmest men I know, was living then all alone in a little cabin on the Klondike, working as a guide for hunting parties. He did not seem to me to have changed much since he took the role of Santa Claus in the school Christmas play in the twenties – a proud, easy-going man, totally independent and, like so many Northerners, quite unflappable. I wonder if I should brave Patsie's wrath this time and get another skin from him.

Behind the store we discover a small museum in front of which stands a remarkable display: the skulls of two moose, locked forever in mortal combat, their huge antlers so inextricably tangled that the battling animals could not withdraw and so died slowly of starvation, staring into each other's eyes. Inside, the shelves are jammed with artifacts found along the Stewart river, all dating back to the goldrush days: dozens of oil lamps of every fashion, gold scales of varying dimension, vintage gramophones, scores of coloured insulators, early tin cans with the labels still affixed and readable, apothecary bottles and spice jars, row upon row—again, an agglomeration of junk that has suddenly become significant.

It is quite possible that some of this discarded packaging might have been left behind by my father's party in the summer of 1898, for they camped on this very spot for several days, taking stock of the situation. Should they travel up the Stewart and look for prospects? (Jack London had spent the previous winter there.) Or should they press on to Dawson? "We put up our tent and unloaded our boats and put out our stuff to dry and hung our bacon," my father reported to his mother. The party had about four tons of goods, enough to last each of them for about a year, but they had not been able to examine the condition of the more perishable provisions since leaving the Stikine. "We found some of our bags badly mouldered. The outside of the flour bags, which were on the bottom as they would be the least damaged by water, were very mouldy from being wet and having no free access to the air. The rest of the things were all right except the tea of which we lost 6 or 8 lbs. out of a 50 lb. chest. We had six 40 lb. bags of oatmeal of which we lost a bag. Several other things were damp but not hurt at all but we dried them out in the sun. After drying everything, we cached the lot."

As usual, he described that cache in meticulous detail. There are several of them standing at Stewart today—little platforms, and sometimes little log cabins, built on stilts, designed to keep away the dogs and wild animals. Like the igloo and the grain elevator, these are unique pieces of Canadian architecture.

But we cannot linger, for we must make camp. A few miles downstream we spy a likely spot. Something long and white lies half hidden in the woods not far from the shoreline; it looks at first like the vertebrae of some prehistoric monster but as we approach it takes on a more familiar contour. It is an old steamboat gangplank lying on its side with shrubs and wildflowers growing through its planking. It takes me back to those days when we used to stand on the shore at places very like this, beside the long piles of cordwood, and watch the deckhands of the *Casca* or the *Whitehorse* running nimbly up the gangplank with their handcarts piled high with birchwood. At the top of the plank each man would pull down on the handles of his cart, pivot expertly in a ninety-degree turn and race down into the bowels of the hold to drop his load with a mighty clatter before returning for another. Now this old gangplank serves our cooks as a workbench on which to spread out food and utensils.

Back in the bush we come upon an oblong clearing large enough to take our tents. It turns out to be the remains of another old road, half obliterated by grasses and sedges but with the ruts still faintly visible. It curves back into the trees and vanishes. How many roads like this lie hidden in the willows and the alders of the Yukon's shoreline, I wonder. Where do they lead? Who came this way and why? Something else catches my eye in the underbrush: the remains of one of the very handcarts used to trundle the cordwood up the gangplank. How I longed to hear that welcome sound of wood clattering into the furnace well during those long days on the mud flats of Dominion creek! I can remember Jim, the big genial boss of the pipeline crew, chuckling and saying to me during that second summer: "Never mind, Pete; it won't be too long now. Pretty soon, you'll be sitting on the deck of that steamboat with a big cigar in your mouth, heading up the river and watching the scenery go by." And then he'd hand me a forty-pound wooden mall and I'd climb up the stepladder and take a few more whacks at the piling we were driving to bedrock to support the pipe that brought down the water that tore up the valley for the dredge the company built. Thus for me the steamboat became the symbol of my future freedom.

It is Skip's birthday eve and in honour of it he is drinking rum and making a salad out of two heads of fresh lettuce from the kitchen garden at Stewart. This is the fourth birthday we have celebrated on the river and there is one more to come. The day we reach Dawson, Peter will turn 17, the same age I was when I went to work on Dominion creek. Much taller than I was then, almost as tall as I am now, he is six foot two and no longer a boy. I realized how swiftly he was growing up last year on the Chilkoot when he and Pamela and I accompanied a group of parks experts making an historical and environmental study of the trail. It was a long hard hike between Sheep Camp and Long lake and in many ways it paralleled the conditions under which my father had climbed the Pass, for he, too, went over it in summer after most of the snow had melted and he had to crawl on hands and knees, as we did, up that forty-five degree incline over a rubble of man-sized boulders, underlaid with shifting shale. We climbed directly into the clouds. A soft mist shrouded us, turning the nearest hikers into shadows, and making the rocks as slippery as if they were sheathed in ice. By the time we reached the summit we were soaked in sweat under our rainwear and totally played out. From this point we could look down the long incline leading to the frozen surface of Crater lake—the very slopes down which my father and his partners sledded their four tons of goods in relays over a period of a week. "I'm sure glad we don't have to do *that*," said Peter, and I agreed. As we moved on he began, for the first time, to ask questions about the grandfather he had never known and in whose footsteps he was following.

Pamela had fallen back with some of the others so Peter and I trudged on together, gasping with fatigue and always aware of the ghostly figure who had preceded us. By the time we came to the end of the day's trek we had each reached our physical limit but of the two, it was clearly the boy who was the fresher. Somebody at the campsite had a flask of brandy and he offered it to us. I passed it to Peter and he took a long grateful gulp and blinked his eyes hard for it was the first raw liquor he had ever swallowed. "Boy, did I need that!" he said, and I thought of the time in the Regina Hotel in Dawson, on the night I arrived for my third summer in the mining camp, when my father had automatically ordered not one, but two hot whiskeys, thus including me, without a word, in the circle of adults at the bar.

"This night Ross and Skip celebrated Skip's birthday," Patsie reports in the logbook. "They were 'tooned,' as Peggy Anne would say. However a merry time was had by all." We sit around the fire once again, singing songs grown familiar from use, reciting Service, drinking hot coffee with rum in it, and all of us getting a little tuned. Peter is included in the adult circle and when he passes his cup across for seconds I remember that evening in the old Regina and refill it for him.

DAY ELEVEN

This will be our last full day on the river and our last night in camp. Because Dawson is less than seventy miles away, we can again enjoy the luxury of drifting for most of the day. The river is a skein of channels and it is not possible for us to float together as we did before. We go our separate ways, some boats choosing one channel, some another; we vanish from each other's sight behind low islands, meet up briefly on the downstream side and separate again. Between the islands the river is sometimes so shallow that the boats scrape the bottom and we have to use our paddles as poles. The Wows, deep in their poker game in The Pig, become so immersed in the play that they allow the boat to drift into a shallow channel and are soon stuck fast on a sandbar, to the great amusement of the rest of us. We watch their struggles through the binoculars as they remove shoes, roll up jeans, climb over the side and try to push the sluggish Pig back into deeper waters. It is a long struggle and no one is going to let the Wows forget it.

Reading my father's brief diary notes, written in pencil in July, 1899, I am struck by incidents and remarks that parallel our excursion. He, too, had been stuck briefly on a sandbar near here. He, too, had broken his journey at Fort Selkirk. On those cramped pages he managed to note the same natural phenomena that have caught my eye: the little sandpipers scuttling along the beaches at Marsh lake; the endless strip of white volcanic ash that extends for miles downstream from Lake Laberge; and the great terraces that vanish once you pass Selkirk. There is one great difference: the cabins and the roads and the placer diggings were less than a year old when he passed this way. And he wrote of meeting other boats all the way down the river and of visiting other camps of goldseekers, many of whom he had known in New Brunswick.

On the right bank somebody spots a small black bear, who is so terrified at the sight of us that he defecates as he scrambles up the hillside. "It made us feel kind of awful." Patsie writes in the log. There is plenty of time for lunch, which means we can dispense with sandwiches and enjoy a hot meal on a sandbar. Pamela has made a big pot of chili, which she heats up on the driftwood fire as we sit in the sunlight watching the river hissing past. How grey it has turned! How measured its pace! Grey, like my father when I saw him on that third and final trip back north to work in the mining camp on Dominion—a shrunken man, moving like a snail down the boardwalk of Fifth Avenue on his way to work, his thinning hair almost white.

He was in his seventieth year and just before I arrived a young doctor had given him some bad advice—or at least that is how it seems to me when I look back on it. He had felt some pains in his chest. The doctor had told him he was suffering from angina pectoris and that he would have to take things easier. Perhaps the doctor did not understand that to my father, a frustrated scientist, the words of a man of science were beyond doubt. He took him literally. Because the doctor had said he must not exert himself, he sold the boat he loved and never again ventured out onto the river. He gave up his walks in the hills. Never again was he to stride up the Old Alaska Commercial Company trail that led to the benchland above, or to follow the white gravel road out to the Bonanza diggings. All this he denied himself. His search for wildflowers ended. When he walked, he walked so slowly that sometimes it seemed as if he was scarcely moving. The doctor had told him that too much exertion would weaken him further; from that moment on, my father was always conscious of the presence of that troubled heart. Nowadays, I suspect, the prescription would not be so drastic: he would be told to exercise moderately and I doubt he would be banned from the river; but in those days doctors knew less about the heart, or at least this one did. Physically, the diagnosis was no doubt accurate; psychologically, it was disastrous. From the moment the doctor gave it, my father was a changed man. When I arrived in Dawson in May I was shocked by his appearance.

This was to be his last summer in the Yukon. My sister was due to arrive the following month to look after him and it was decided that in the fall we would take the steamboat back up the river for the last time together. My father was convinced that he lived under sentence of death.

For me that third season on Dominion creek was not as gruelling as the two before. We had good bunkhouses, better food, hot showers and a nine-hour day. Now I was working with men closer to my own age, though I was still the youngest on the job. More important, I had grown older and physically tougher and the work did not wholly exhaust me. In the evenings, instead of tumbling into bed, I played poker with my fellow workers and even put out a camp newspaper, pinned up once a week on the bulletin board. Sometimes, a bunch of us would walk down to the old roadhouse at Paris—a roadhouse that had been in operation since the goldrush days—and drink bootleg rum with the proprietor,

George Fraser, who had lived there since 1898 and would die there without ever venturing so far as Dawson. ("Dawson's too much for me," he used to say. "Too many bright lights.") Once, to celebrate the longest day of the year, I stayed out all night, got roaring drunk and walked ten miles back to camp just in time to stagger down to work without breakfast. It did not faze me; it seemed that as my father lost energy I gained – almost as if nature had allotted us a finite amount to be divided up according to our years.

My mother was waiting for us on the dock at Vancouver that fall and I saw the sudden look of alarm in her face as my father slowly made his way down the gangplank.

"The suitcases," he was saying, "has somebody got the suitcases?"

"Don't worry," I said. "I'll handle that."

"Yes," said my mother, giving me a strange look, "you handle everything."

Forty-one years had passed since he first came through the same city as a young man. "It is not much of a place, about 20,000 inhabitants," he had written to his mother from Vancouver. "There are a few fine buildings and the principal streets are paved with asphalt. Most sidewalks are wood with some flagstones. There are a great many Chinese. . . ." Dawson in those days was a much bigger town than Vancouver and some of its buildings were more imposing but in the intervening forty-one years Vancouver had grown twenty-fold while Dawson had shrunk by the same multiple. It occurs to me now, as we float down the silent river, that I am one of the few Canadians raised in a community where growth was not the norm, where real estate dropped instead of rising, where completely furnished houses could be snapped up for a trifle, and where the town, instead of expanding into suburbs and spilling over its own limits, shrank in upon itself – the satellite settlements across the two rivers shrivelling and withering until they were no more, and the edges of the old city blurring as the sidewalks on the outskirts atrophied and fell into disuse and the buildings wasted away and the invading willows and alders crept like a disease over the abandoned lawns and gardens. As a child I had thought all towns were like that. I was so used to boarded-up buildings tottering in the permafrost and to empty cabins collapsing in the bushes that it did not strike me that this was decay until I returned to Dawson many years later and saw it with new eyes. To a boy raised in a ghost town, the Boom is something that belongs to the past and not to the future.

We intend to make camp at the last of the historic settlements on the river route to Dawson. This is the pre-goldrush trading post of Ogilvie, on an island opposite the mouth of the Sixtymile river – so named by the early traders because it was sixty miles upstream from the original Yukon river trading post at Fort Reliance. Among the earliest traders was a New Yorker of French-Canadian stock, a veteran of the river since 1882 named Joseph Ladue. One of the log buildings now fallen into disrepair on this island must have been his original post.

There are a good many vacant cabins at Ogilvie; we find them clustered in two groups separated by a shallow slough that partially divides the island. We move the boats into the shelter of the slough and, in a light rain, make camp in the very heart of the old settlement.

Here, again, is where history was made. It was from this spot that Robert Henderson was grubstaked by Ladue in the mid-Nineties to prospect the Indian river country. Ladue felt there was gold somewhere on the headwaters of the Indian–on Quartz or Sulphur or Dominion creeks–and of course events proved him right. Having probed the Indian, Henderson turned his attention to the neighbouring watershed of the Klondike. It was, then, from this very beach that Chester Henderson's grandfather pushed off in the summer of 1896 with fresh supplies from Ladue's trading post for his memorable meeting with George Carmack–a meeting that led to the strike that touched off the great mass movement known as the Klondike stampede. As we climb out of the boats I can visualize the two men standing here: Henderson, gaunt, lean and rugged, stepping into his poling boat and Ladue, swarthy and enthusiastic, waving him off and telling him not to worry about his bill. In those days a prospector's credit was unlimited.

My father stopped here briefly in August, 1898, just two years later. He and some of his party had decided to take the canoe, a tent, and a fortnight's provisions and have a look at Dawson "to find out what is to be found out," as he put it, before deciding whether to prospect the Stewart or come on downriver with all the gear. "We passed on our way Sixtymile Post opposite Sixtymile river, where the trader had quite a garden. Potatoes in flower, cabbages, lettuce, turnips, beans, radishes and beets. He had lost a good deal in the spring by the freshet and the ice carrying away part of his crop but the remainder was doing well. In fact the climate here has been very much misrepresented. A finer summer climate one could not wish to see." These last words were meant to reassure his mother, who believed him to be swallowed up in a land of perpetual snow.

There is no sign of that garden now, except for some vagrant delphiniums springing out of the grass. The encroaching forest has long since obliterated any sign of a clearing in the woods. As for the buildings, they, too, are rapidly returning to the soil. "The guy's house had fallen in," Patsie writes in the log. "But it was really neat seeing his old two-holer and his wallpaper and neat old imported door. There were remnants of milk cartons and other old supplies. . . . The other cabins were also falling apart and an eerie feeling prevailed. There was a lot of little things, so it seemed as if Ladue suddenly took up and left when the next boat came through. There were harnesses, sacks of sawdust, mattresses, Jehovah's Witnesses books, files and good tools, cans of spices that still smelled the same, pots and pans, washboard, paper [news] and a chair. . . ."

These, of course, would not have been left behind by Ladue. He turned his post over to others and set off for the Klondike's mouth as soon as he heard of the gold strike. He did not dig for gold like the others. Instead he laid out a townsite and set up a sawmill, for Ladue, the trader, knew that the real gold would be garnered by a man shrewd enough to have the only supply of sluice-box planking in the Yukon. His Ogilvie post thrived for many years after the stampede and some of the newspapers here are dated as recently as December, 1930. "Babe Ruth thinks he's worth $85,000 a year . . . " one of the stories begins. That, I remember, was the last winter I ever spent in the Yukon.

It is my turn to do the cooking. The menu for Day Eleven says clam chowder and so I go to work with tinned clams, condensed milk and all the left-over bacon. Meanwhile, Pamela and Patsie are determined to bake a birthday cake for Skip. They fashion an oven of sorts out of an old gasoline tin found in one of the cabins and place a flat pan of Brownie mix inside it. This goes at the edge of the fire and everybody hopes for the best. The result is passable if some-what crumbly, and slightly burned on the bottom. After we

154

devour the chowder, they present the cake to Skip with a candle made of wood sticking in the middle. "He had to blow like hell to get it out," Patsie comments in the log. Meanwhile Ross Miller, who has known Skip since that first Boy Scout trip down the Yukon, is preparing a presentation. I have only just realized that Ross is 18 years old; with his dark beard and his voluminous knowledge of glacial science, gained from his father, he seems more like 26. His gift to Skip is a plaque fashioned from a tin can lid, on which he has engraved with his hunting knife, the following citation:

FOR UNDYING PERSEVERANCE
IN THE FACE OF UNRELENTING BERTONS
THE GRIN-AND-BEAR-IT HAPPY-HONEYMOON
NEVER-AGAIN AWARD PRESENTED TO
ROBERT RIVERRUNNER

Aug. 15, 1972   Wowgilvie
                        Yukon Territory

Ross ties the medal to Peggy Anne's pyjama belt and hangs it around Skip's neck as we all applaud and sing Happy Birthday.

The time has come to start throwing things away. Janet and Pamela have a tendency to save everything—from tins of bacon fat to half-empty packets of Betty Crocker mix. The gastronomic story of our river trip is to be found in the left-overs and the disposal of the dead weight brings its own nostalgia. *Look at those biscuits: remember how wet we got in the lakes? Remember Dad's puffballs? Remember the fake moosemeat at Bennett? Remember when Peter caught the first grayling? We really wowed out over that one! Don't throw away the beans—they were real good!*

It is hard to believe that the great adventure, which we have been planning for most of the year, is almost at an end. It seems only hours ago that we were setting out from Lake Bennett, marvelling at the mountains. But the river, we realize, moves more swiftly than we thought and home is only a few miles past the next bend.

DAY TWELVE

Patsie describes our last morning in the log: "We planned to get to Dawson by noon, so we had a 'quick' breakfast of coffee and Penny's famous perverse mucilage [Patsie's name for the Swiss health cereal, *Bierscher Muesli*] and used up the remaining (!!arg!) dried fruit. Then Big Pierre starts chucking out all the extra food supplies that weren't needed. . . . P.S. Dad called Betty Crocker a witch and burned all the Twinkle mixes and other useless things in the fire and Mum was running round and grabbing and snatching things to save as Dad cursed her for being squirrel-like."

At last we are packed. The boats push off down the little slough and out into the main river and some of the children begin to sing a verse of an old Yukon folk song I taught them years ago, which begins with the phrase: "It's twenty miles from Dawson and times are awful tough." We are about fifty-five miles from Dawson and we have only one more stop to make on the way. Patsie describes it in the log:

"We cruised up to a friend of Skip's place—Pete and Mary's. They were living in an old trapper's cabin, roughing it in the bush. Mary was only there, looking like she'd lived there all summer, really peaceful and full of energy and smiles. She seemed to really dig living out there and planned to live there for a long time, always if possible, living with

157

her husband, Pete, future children and dogs. They trap in the winter. The area is reasonably hilly, not mountains, but there are lots of trees. Anyway I found it really a beautiful way of living and an incredible place."

They are a very young couple, indeed—from California, I think. Some people might once have called them hippies. They have bought a trapline from an old timer and have learned the business, I suppose, by trial and error. There is a flock of handsome husky dogs, all going insane at the end of their chains, a good garden and a greenhouse rigged up of plastic and full of ripening tomatoes. I think of my own parents, starting out in much the same way, though they lacked the stereo sound system and eight-track cartridges that bring the voices of Joni and Jimi to the wilderness. What a boon those tapes must be in the long night of mid-winter!

The freight canoe has encountered engine trouble and Scotty will have to drift into town, but the rest of us are eager to reach our destination and decide to use the motors. For me, the scenery is becoming more and more familiar. On our right, I spot the mouth of the Indian river, some twenty miles upstream from Dawson. That was about as far as the *Bluenose* could go in a day if we were to get home by midnight, so it has connotations of excitement for me, since excursions to the Indian river were necessarily few. The islands now begin to take on remembered contours, though they have changed so much over more than forty years that it is difficult to tell which were the ones we camped on. But Chicken Billy's island, which was one of our favourites, is unmistakeable and so is the mouth of Swede creek and the little slough at Sunnydale, where the hay farm used to be.

Now, rising behind the intervening bluff, I can see the familiar pyramid shape of the Midnight Dome. The bluff ends at the Klondike flats, the site of Klondike City, better known as Lousetown. In my day there were the remains of an old brewery and a sawmill here and many cabins, including the "cribs" of the goldrush prostitutes, some of them still occupied. Now there is nothing. The wilderness has reclaimed Lousetown and this bank of the Klondike must look very much as it did in the days before the goldrush when it was a salmon stream and not an Eldorado.

In front of us, as we sweep around the great bluff, the old town lies spread out along the right bank for about a mile. Years ago it stretched for a mile and a half but age has caused it to shrink. The gaps where buildings once stood are more pronounced, great blank areas covered in bush or grass and empty spaces between buildings that once were crowded along Front Street. The old police barracks is in good shape, because the Historic Sites and Monuments Board uses it as a headquarters. St. Paul's church, where my mother sang, is freshly painted. But dancehall row is no more: the old Orpheum, the Monte Carlo, the M & N, Apple Jimmy's, the Flora Dora and Dominion Gambling House—all of these historic structures which survived to my day have since been burned in one of Dawson's innumerable fires. (I think again of my father waiting protectively in the movie house.) St. Mary's Hospital, built by Father Judge, "the Saint of Dawson," where I almost died of pneumonia at the age of two, is long gone, too; indeed the whole north end is a decaying shambles, returning to scrub bush. But one brown old building still remains and on its side we can make out the faint letters LADUE SAWMILL COMPANY.

We bring our boats into a little beach just below the Bank of Commerce—the same bank where Robert Service once worked as a teller weighing gold until he was dismissed because he was making more money from his poetry than the manager made from banking. The bank, an Edwardian structure sheathed in galvanized iron, has been freshly painted and behind it, perched on the beach in tip-top condition for the tourist trade, is the restored steamboat *Keno* on which my friend Hambone once worked as a steward.

The smaller children begin to scamper about in excitement.

"Why, it's like an old-fashioned town!" Peggy Anne exclaims, looking up the street at the old frame buildings, with their cornices and fretwork, their bay windows and overhanging balconies. I am startled by her delight, which contrasts with my own despair. I am seeing Dawson now through four pairs of eyes. I see it as my father first saw it when it was in its prime: the biggest city west of Winnipeg and north of San Francisco, with running water, electric lights and motion pictures, with the buildings spanking new, the streets crowded with men from all over the globe, the restaurants serving oyster dinners while string orchestras played the classics, and the dancehalls, the gambling houses and the saloons roaring full blast day and night. I see it as I remember it from my boyhood: a very ordinary town no different as far as I knew from any other town – rather, in fact, like the small towns I used to read about in Booth Tarkington's novels, complete with dusty roads and shady walks, neat, flower-decked cottages and pretty, steepled churches, with horses clip-clopping down the main street and the river running past our front door. I see it as it looks to me now, through the eyes of a returning native: shrivelled, faded and apparently dying – so many shattered windows, so many boarded-up doors, so many gardens abandoned to the weeds, so many wooden sidewalks smothered by the invading alders. Last, I see it through the eyes of my children: a quaint storybook town, a fossilized piece of the past, romantic

in its old age, even charming in its decay—a sort of Disney-
land here in the Yukon, except that nothing is made up,
everything is real, all is history.

Skip has a minibus to take us and our gear to the hotel—
not one of the hotels of my childhood but a new motel
called the Eldorado, complete with cocktail lounge, running
water and keys for the doors. The old hotels are all gone.
The Occidental across the way, better known as The Bucket
of Blood, has been boarded up. So has the old Principal
down the street. The Central is gone; the Royal Alexandra
is gone; the Regina is gone; the Yukonia is gone. They were
all of a piece, these hotels: the ceilings of stamped-out metal,
the floors of worn linoleum, with circular black leather set-
tees, the potted ferns, the spittoons with dead cigars floating
in them, the polished desk with the mustached clerk in
striped shirt and armbands, the big register book, the stair-
case winding up to the rooms that never needed a key, the
chipped china basin and jug, the great brass-knobbed bed,
the single bathroom down the hall, the polished mahogany
bar downstairs, the back room with its inevitable poker
game, the big doors that never closed. I drank my first Tom
Collins in one of these hotels at the age of 19, to celebrate
the end of my last season in a mining camp; it cost fifty
cents, which was an hour's wages in 1939, and it was technically illegal. But if a hotel man had a beer licence it was
tacitly agreed that he could sell anything and all of them did.

Now, behind our locked doors in the Pembroke baths of
the Eldorado, we sluice a week of Yukon dust from our
bodies to emerge in store clothes, well-scrubbed and barely
recognizable. A man from the Historic Sites and Monuments
Board is waiting in the lobby for me. He does not seem to
have changed greatly since the days when we Wolf Cubs
cooked our beans on the hills above the town—a little greyer,

161

perhaps, and a bit heavier, but as calm and unruffled as ever. John Gould, whose mother made the best baked beans in Dawson, is now in charge of a multi-million dollar plan to restore some of the buildings in whose shadow we both were raised. He talks about it matter-of-factly. The old Palace Grand dancehall was the first. Now the original post office is being repaired. After that, probably, Mme. Tremblay's old store. Who would have thought of Mme. Tremblay's store as a monument? To us it was a place where, during Christmas week, you could look in the lighted windows and see the mechanical toys you hoped somebody would give you for Christmas. Now the store is to be preserved and its owner, long deceased, to be immortalized. She was, it turns out, the first woman to cross the Chilkoot Pass, years before the goldrush. I had never known that; to me she was a motherly creature, with white hair and a French accent. But her story and that of her store have already been detailed in a plaque displayed on the building. Later, other buildings will be preserved with the help of John Gould, whose even temperament and obvious good health are a tribute to his mother's cooking.

The children are already noticing something about Northerners—that they are shaped to a different mould by climate, loneliness, environment and heritage. More than once Patsie in the log has referred to the inner serenity of the wilderness people. Almost everybody who visits Dawson talks about the special quality of the old timers. Part of it comes, I think, from a kind of personal security which is the stamp of those who have survived and prospered in a harsh environment; some of it springs out of the very isolation of the northern communities, which forces the people to fall back on their own resources (we notice the absence of television aerials in Dawson); some of it comes from the need to co-operate for survival rather than to compete – the tradition of the open cabin door goes back before the stampede. It is difficult to bamboozle Northerners. Phoneys they can spot a mile away. Fads, fashions and sudden enthusiasms are not for them. They suffer no identity crises. Men like John Gould know exactly who they are and where their roots are and so they do not find it necessary to play a role or wear a costume.

The wooden sidewalks of the old town beckon. We leave John Gould and set off on a tour of exploration and of re-discovery. The Red Feather Saloon is kitty-corner from the motel and across the street, Billy Biggs' blacksmith shop is long disused but still standing. I can remember when it rang to the sound of hammer and anvil, the sparks flying out from the dark interior, while we boys sat for hours watching the horses from the neighbouring livery stable being shod. Most of Third Avenue seems to have retreated into the weeds. The flower gardens, once Dawson's pride, have almost all disappeared. If the town is to be restored it must be done quickly. The old gun shop, certainly the most photographed building in the Yukon, is literally falling apart and has had to be propped up with poles on the outside and steel beams within. It will take some doing to preserve it in one piece.

Walking past these buildings I cannot help but think of my father, fading gently away in the last six years of his life in Vancouver. It was as if his real existence ended after he left the Yukon. Slowly he began to lose interest in the things that used to excite him: mathematics, the classics, his garden, the Royal Astronomical Society, contract bridge, and finally, even his loom. He took to reading cheap detective novels, one after another, while the *Scientific American* lay untouched in the magazine rack. It was if he were holding a waiting brief for death. "It's not likely you'll be seeing me again," he'd say, every time I said goodbye to him at the end of my various army leaves. Yet he hung on, growing weaker but never desperately ill, until the very end of the war. When I came back from overseas in the summer of 1945 he was bed-ridden and it was clear that his life was struggling towards its close. We took turns sitting up with him at night, my mother, my sister and I, sleeping on a little cot in his room — for he could no longer look after himself. For some of this time, especially in the nights, he was half-delirious. Once I heard him call out in anguish: "Matchsticks! Matchsticks!" I could not fathom what he meant. "Matchsticks! Match-sticks!" my father cried again and then looking up, from my pillow, I saw him gazing down at his legs, the blankets flung aside. They were indeed as thin as matchsticks, these withered limbs, once as thick as tree trunks, that had carried him over mountains and across the Yukon hills and which, when he was 46 years old, had outmarched those of soldiers half his age.

But still he did not die, though he clearly expected to. Night after night he used to gather his family around him for the deathbed scene which, with his love of ritual and his knowledge of history, he wanted so badly to enact. That was how men died in books. That was how kings died. But this neat, romantic ending — this final satisfaction — was to be denied him.

"It's an awful thing to have to say," my mother said to me when I returned from overseas, "but, oh God, I wish he would die! Is that so terrible? To wish that for him?"

It was not terrible, for we all wished him to be out of his pain — pain that even morphine could not relieve. When my month's overseas leave ended he was still alive. Although the war was over the army did not acknowledge that fact and I was shipped off to the prairies to learn jungle warfare in order to fight an enemy who no longer existed. And there, in August, I got a wire from my mother urging me to come home because my father had been taken to the hospital. I was given compassionate leave and caught the next train to the coast.

In the CPR station in Vancouver I bought a morning paper and read it while waiting for the streetcar. As I passed the classified advertising section, a name caught my eye. It was my father's. It headed the obituary column and, reading the details in the agate type, I felt only an immense wave of relief that it was over.

"It was his heart that kept him alive," my mother told me when I reached home. "It's ironic, isn't it? Everything else went, apparently–his circulation . . . everything. It's all in the autopsy. It was his heart that wouldn't stop beating. The one thing he thought would kill him turned out to be the strongest part of him."

The Administration Building, where he worked for a quarter of a century, still stands in Minto Park. It is a handsome structure, in a design which might be labelled frontier classical. Much of it has fallen into disrepair since the government offices were moved to Whitehorse but part of it has been converted into an historical museum. For me, as for my family, this is a place of endless fascination. Every kind of memento is to be found here, from bits of mining machinery to old scrapbooks. The Dawson that I knew and that my parents knew is preserved here in artifact and photograph. There are photographs of the town in its very first days as a tent community; photographs of the great days, when it was jammed with cabins and warehouses and a dozen steamboats and hundreds of small craft lined the river bank;

photographs of Dawson as I knew her in her fading elegance with fretworked public buildings and cottages with wide verandahs. Here, for instance is a photograph of a house I often played in, that of the RCMP inspector; it stands to this day, across from the museum, but it is a total ruin. Here is a photograph of the Discovery Day parade in the 1920s, showing the long line of goldrush pioneers, my father among them, wearing the gold and purple sashes of the Yukon Order of Pioneers and heading off to Minto Park where Mr. Schwartz was preparing to dole out free soda pop. Here are photographs of all the old steamboats, and the railway trains that once ran out to Bonanza creek, and the great costume ball where my sister went dressed as Bo-Peep and I as Little Boy Blue. Here is the school we went to, now torn down and here is a photograph of the first airplane into Dawson, the *Queen of the Yukon*. Here is a photograph of a snowshoe party taken before World War One and at the far left of the group stands a slender woman in a fashionable long skirt and toque; I recognize those solemn, brown eyes which I see again in my own children and in her grandson Berton. Here she is, ten years later, in a photograph of the Imperial Order of the Daughters of the Empire; the face has a few lines on it, but the eyes are still large and solemn. And here, in an album showing all the children born in St. Mary's Hospital, is a photograph of an equally solemn little girl with those same brown eyes and I explain to Berton that this is his mother, pictured at the age of two. For him this whole experience is more moving than it is for my offspring, since he knew his grandmother much better than they did. She lived a few blocks away and used to tell him stories, all through his boyhood, about the strange town in the north where his mother was raised. For all of his life he has seen this town in his mind and he tells me now that in one way it is exactly as he imagined it—for my mother's descriptions were nothing if not graphic—and in another way it is oddly different. But then she was describing Dawson as it was almost half a century before.

I leave the children to pore through the albums and I walk out of the museum and across the hall to the disused wing of the Administration Building. Two boards nailed across the doorway block my entrance but, looking through into the big room beyond, I see what I have come to see. The ceiling has partly fallen in and the room is littered with debris. The lines have been blurred by dust and cobwebs. The big carts of mining files have long since been removed to Whitehorse and the doors of the old vaults hang open, but his desk is there, covered with rubble but intact, the desk at which he worked for twenty-five years. I can see him again . . . the vest . . . the armlets . . . the green eyeshade . . . and the two small children, riding on the carts into the vault and then taking him by the hand at closing time to lead him up the steep hill to home.

The rest of the family troop out of the museum and we all leave the building and walk across the little park with its white obelisk, marking the dead of World War One. I look towards the rear of the Administration Building and feel that something seems to be missing. What is it? The place seems strangely naked. Then a recurring dream comes back to me, a dream that I have had for many decades, a dream in which I am scampering and hiding between rows of tall wooden walls behind a familiar building I cannot identify. Now I realize that this is that building and those walls were high stacks of cordwood arranged in parallel lines and stretching out like fingers behind the back door of my father's office, where we children often played in the afternoons after school.

The park seems to have shrunk. It used to take me a long time to cross it, or so it seemed; now we reach its borders in a few paces. Part of it has been appropriated for a new hospital, designed in a style I call Territorial Modern. We are cutting across the lawn near Seventh Avenue when a man comes out from behind the building and shouts: "Hey! Where do you get off stepping all over my grass?" I am about to apologize when I notice that he is grinning at me and as he approaches I recognize him. He no longer has the horns or the tail but otherwise he has not changed greatly since that Sunday morning at Apple Jimmy's fruit stand. Like John Gould and Chester Henderson, Axel Nordling has remained in his home town. In fact he has now lived in Dawson longer than my father did; he can, however, escape each winter to the Mexican or the Hawaiian sun – the airplane has made that possible. We talk about the rest of the gang, many long departed, some still in the North. I will see a few of them at the Pioneer Dance tomorrow night. But I will not see Chester Henderson nor will I be able to buy another grizzly rug from him at his cabin along the Klondike. He was found there last year, dead by his own hand. He was incurably ill and it was not in his nature to allow himself to be a charge on any man.

We leave Axel and walk up the little road which used to bear the name of Joseph Ladue's partner, Arthur Harper, and down whose steep slopes I used to coast in the small wagon my father bought me for my seventh birthday. How gentle that slope seems now! How narrow the roadway! At the top, on Eighth Avenue and just under the hill, is the little cabin where Robert Service wrote his second volume of verse. Across from it is a tiny cottage now identified as part of the Robert Service Motel. The canary vine, which used to smother it at this time of year, no longer grows here but the briar roses are still blooming near the front door and the birches and cottonwoods which always lined the borders of the front yard seem scarcely to have changed. I realize, with a start, that these are not the same trees but the offspring of those I knew as a child. And there is the verandah on which I slept and contemplated, each summer, the mystery of the stars; and there is the addition my father built when the family began to grow up. And there, propping it up like flying buttresses, are the long poles used everywhere in Dawson to support decaying buildings.

There is no one living in the house. We borrow a key and enter through the kitchen. To me it seems oddly distorted, like a house revisited in a dream. The rooms seem tiny, built for dwarves. Can this really be the spacious hallway of my boyhood? I can hardly turn around in it. Did four of us actually sleep in this cubicle of a bedroom? Did this diminutive yard I see from the little kitchen window actually hold the gigantic garden of memory? Nothing has changed yet everything has changed. The familiar furniture, my father's books, the circular dining room table, the dentist's chair in the den, the lamp he made as a present for my mother, the copies of the *Scientific American,* his fur coat and hat hanging next to his walking stick in the hall, my sister's dolls, my own mechanical toys, the Haynes Brothers piano, the old Remington on which my mother's novel was written – all these are gone. The house is a shell from which the spirit has flown and, like the road outside and the garden below and the town itself, half hidden by the invading wilderness, it seems to have shrunk, like an old man withering away on his deathbed, his sinews atrophied and his limbs as thin as matchsticks.

LAST DAY

We are standing in a group on the top of the Midnight Dome high above the town. It is August 17, the Discovery Day of old, now celebrated on the previous weekend in the fashion of most Canadian holidays "so that the town can enjoy a three-day drunk" as one native put it to me. But the Yukon Order of Pioneers will celebrate it with an Old Time Dance tonight and we will all go.

We have come up on Skip's minibus to this highest point above the town to enjoy a picnic and see the Yukon and Klondike valleys spread out below us and look at the view, which is one of the most magnificent in all the Yukon. We have come up past Thomas Gulch, where I once thought myself lost, and past the Moosehide Trail, where, fifty years ago this month, my mother and I ate toffee rolls, and past the cemeteries which stretch out on the hillside – hundreds and hundreds of graves, with half the names obliterated and great trees poking up through the mounds – and past the old farms where we used to play in the hay, long since given over again to the wild, and up above the treeline to this windswept peak overlooking both the rivers and the famous gold creeks and the community of Dawson.

From this distance one gets the illusion of gazing back in time. The town below us looks almost new. The streets criss-crossing one another at neat, geometric angles give it the appearance of a modern suburb; one cannot see the crumbling sidewalks or the intruding weeds, while the blank spaces appear as parks and the buildings, from above, do not seem to be falling down.

Out on the grey breast of the Yukon, Captain Dick Stevenson's little sternwheeler, *Yukon Lou*, takes its quota of tourists downriver to the empty Indian village of Moosehide and across to the old shipyard where the *Susie* and the *Schwatka* and the *Julia B.* have laid their bones. What saddens me, excites the visitors. They have never seen a steamboat before and these decaying sternwheelers are the stuff of history. If Dick Stevenson has his way, a new boat, perhaps as big as the *Julia B.*, may soon be cruising the river. Every year more and more Outsiders pour into Dawson, which in its old age – and perhaps because of its old age – has again become a mecca.

Below me I can see the original post office, with its Edwardian cupola, now propped up and refurbished by federal funds, under John Gould's management. Mme. Tremblay's is just across the street and a few doors away towards the river stands the first of the restored buildings, the magnificent opera house which Arizona Charley Meadows built in 1899 and called the Palace Grand. Each summer night it is filled with people from the Outside who drive up the highway to visit the cabins where Service wrote his poems and where Jack London spent a winter. The further the goldrush fades into the past, the more the tourists are captivated by it.

The machinery that used to line the streets and the river bank has vanished. But some of it, repainted, has been arranged in an outdoor museum by George Shaw, the jeweller. There you can see the old stage sleigh my mother took on that winter journey back to Dawson, and the pilot's cabin from the steamboat *Nasutlin* and the original steam pumper from the Dawson fire hall, which I remember so well, and a variety of mining equipment—all the pieces of junk from my era now labelled and displayed as historical curiosities. There are at least three museums operating in Dawson now and probably many more to come. For the town, in its decay, has taken on an aura; dying it may be and yet its heart continues to beat; there is nothing else like it in Canada and those who visit it are charmed as my children are charmed.

"Oh, Dad, can't we stay a few days longer?" Peggy Anne asks. "*Please*, Dad?"

"Don't worry," I tell them. "You'll be back." There is no doubt about that now.

And so we sit on top of the Dome and drink our beer and eat our sandwiches, as my family used to do when I was small. There is something missing—a sound once borne upon the wind. No longer do I hear the far-off screaming of the gold dredges, pivoting restlessly on their great anchors. That indescribable whine was created by the action of taut cables rasping against pulleys but to an imaginative boy it sounded like a thousand souls in torment. Today there is only the roar of the Klondike pouring across its gravel bed to join the larger river.

I point it out to them, the most famous river in the North, stretching back into the hills. In the distance we can see Bonanza creek wriggling off to the wooded horizon, choked with old gravel tailings, its flanks gored by hydraulic works. Beyond that is the King Dome and beyond it, Dominion creek, where I once worked and Quigley Gulch, where my father built his cabin. All of this has become historic country; the gravel piles, the hydraulic cuts, the old diggings, the great, sunken dredge, the bits of machinery lying in the shallow creeks, the famous benches—French Hill, Gold Hill, Cheechako Hill—the claims along Eldorado, each of which yielded a million dollars or more; all have become valuable in themselves through the passage of time.

"*I'd* sure like to come back," one of the children says. "Maybe work here for a couple of years."

A couple of years! My father had come, intending to stay just a couple of years.

"Yeah, maybe you could work as a tourist guide."

Will the tourist industry spark a new goldrush? I look down at Dawson through half-closed eyes and again try to see it as it was when I was a boy and as it was when my father first saw it. And then I try to imagine it as it may look when the main buildings are restored and the whole town and the creeks beyond become a kind of gigantic historical museum. It will not then be the town I knew or the town my parents knew or, indeed, the town it is today; for all I know, the Dawson of tomorrow may be crammed with chicken palaces and root beer drive-ins and flashing neon signs and things that buzz and rotate.

Nevertheless, certain characteristics will endure. There is a continuity in communities as there is in families. I doubt if there is anyone left alive who experienced the goldrush, but there are many who have experienced the men who experienced the goldrush. On the streets of Dawson I have run into several people who knew my parents. "Your father lent me money once," one old man said to me yesterday. "Told me not to say anything about it." "Your mother taught me kindergarten" another told me. "I was in her very first class." And another: "I still remember the day your father tried to tell me how the Northern Lights worked—how patient he was." And a fourth: "You know I've still got the tooth he filled? Didn't hurt either and he gave me a free swallow of brandy."

It is beginning to rain. The children are reluctant to leave because this really is the end. We must say goodbye to Dawson and also to Skip and Cheri and Scotty and Ross. It is strange to think that Skip will be back down the river again in a matter of weeks with another party and will again be standing here on the Dome overlooking Dawson.

As the children climb into the bus ("We'll all write you, Skip!" "Don't lose our addresses!" "Don't forget to send the photographs"), I take one last look. Here, on the Dome, we seem to be on top of the world, the land stretching off for miles below us. Upriver, the sun is shining through the rain, mottling the green hills and gleaming in patches on the water. The Yukon, unchanged and unchanging, coils out of the south the way we have come and swings under the Dawson bluffs and around the town, and then winds north, growing wider in the distance, its bright ribbon glittering like silver in the strange light, its teardrop islands half hidden in the soft mist that rises from the water. You can see for a long way from the top of the Dome – ridge after ridge of hills, blue in the foreground, violet in the middle ground, hazy in the distance – but you cannot see where the river will end. Our own odyssey is over, but the river's has only begun.